Harvest for the World

Harvest for the World

A Christian Aid/CAFOD worship anthology
on sharing in the work of creation

Compiled by Geoffrey Duncan

for  **Christian Aid**

and **CAFOD**
just one world

CANTERBURY
PRESS
Norwich

© in this compilation Geoffrey Duncan 2002, 2004

First published in 2002 by the Canterbury Press Norwich
(a publishing imprint of Hymns Ancient & Modern Limited,
a registered charity)
St Mary's Works, St Mary's Plain,
Norwich, Norfolk NR3 3BH

Second Edition 2004

www.scm-canterburypress.co.uk

British Library Cataloguing in Publication data

A catalogue record for this book is available
from the British Library

ISBN 1-85311-574-6

Typeset by Rowland Phototypesetting Limited,
Bury St Edmunds, Suffolk
Printed in Great Britain by Biddles Limited,
www.biddles.co.uk

Contents

Foreword

Harvest for many of us can appear something of an irrelevance. Now that global trade brings us all kinds of foods all the year round, those of us who live in towns and cities easily lose sight of the natural cycle of seedtime and harvest on which the growers of our food depend. As a result, traditional harvest festival celebrations, at least in urban areas, may have an air of unreality about them. We don't ourselves 'plough the fields and scatter the good seed on the land', and many of us rarely see other people doing that either. Canned foods and material goods seem to be more appropriate gifts to send to a school or church service for thanksgiving than the traditional offerings of fruit and flowers, which nowadays few city-dwellers can, or want to, grow themselves.

In rural areas, though, harvest is as important as ever, as many farmers struggle to make a living in a market dominated by big business looking to sell cheaply rather than buy fairly. And in many developing countries, where agricultural subsidies and other forms of assistance just don't exist, individuals and communities depend for their very survival on a good – or at least a reasonable – harvest. More than any other season of the year, harvest is a time that highlights contrasts: between rich consumers and poor producers; between people for whom the countryside is to be enjoyed from a speeding car, and others whose livelihood depends on fertile soil, healthy animals, and the right mix of sun and rain.

Following the successful collaboration in which CAFOD joined Christian Aid and Canterbury Press in publishing the anthology for Lent, Holy Week and Easter, *Let Justice Roll Down*, Geoffrey Duncan has now produced an expanded edition of *Harvest for the World*, which incorporates material from a more Catholic tradition. This new edition offers a still wider range of harvest material for use in a variety of contexts. Writers from around the world encourage us to celebrate familiar and less familiar aspects of God's creation. Stories and poems, many of them relating to the work of Christian Aid's and CAFOD's partners overseas, tell of people's hopes and achievements in unpromising circumstances.

Some contributions reflect the growing campaign for justice in world trade, a theme which is particularly well suited to harvest. The responsibility of those of us who live in rich countries is highlighted in Kathleen Scullion's prayer:

Lord,
Open our eyes to the need for fairness,
Open our eyes to the cries of the people.
Open our hearts to a greater understanding,
Open our lips to share the truth.

Give us the courage to speak out.
Give us the confidence to confront the powerful.
Give us the strength to persevere.
Be with us, Lord, as we strive to create a fairer world.

Like this one, the pieces in this anthology can be used in harvest worship or at virtually any other time when it is appropriate to reflect on today's world. For groups holding special harvest meals there is a selection of blessings and graces, as well as a few recipes from various parts of the world to help produce a harvest supper with a difference.

However you choose to use this anthology, it will be a rich addition to more traditional harvest resources, reminding us as it does of our dependence on one another and on God. In the words of this prayer from the Ethiopian Orthodox Church:

From all evil works keep us apart,
And in all good works unite us.
You are life for our souls.
You are the life of the world.

Paula Clifford
Christian Aid

Part One:

For the beauty of the earth . . .

'And God saw all that he had made,
and it was very good.'
Genesis 1:31

Come, Come Away (Creation's Song)

Based on Song of Songs 2:10–13, 16–17

O come, come away, for the winter is past;
The rain now is over and flowers bloom at last:
Here's laughter for weeping and colour for grey;
O rise up, my fair one; my love, come away.

O sing, sing for joy, for the time is at hand;
The turtle-dove calls once again through our land:
Here's laughter for weeping and colour for grey;
O rise up, my fair one; my love, come away.

O come, on the fig tree there's fruit to be found;
The blossoming vine spreads its fragrance around;
Here's laughter for weeping and colour for grey;
O rise up, my fair one; my love, come away.

Love, love is mine and to love I belong;
Till day breathes anew and the shadows are gone:
Here's laughter for weeping and colour for grey;
O rise up, my fair one; my love, come away.

Jenny Dann

Thanksgiving

For the gift of creation:
For the enormous: for the tiny,
For refreshment: for a challenge,
For gentle beauty: for fierce beauty,

3

For all the variety of place and season,
For fruitfulness,
        We praise you.

For the inheritance in creation, from generations past:
        For landscape,
        For craft and skill,
        For breed and variety in livestock and crops,
        For wildlife untamed,
        For fertility maintained,
                We praise you.

For our existence in creation:
        For air,
        For space,
        For moisture,
        For food,
                We praise you.

For those who represent us all in tending creation:
        For gardeners,
        For foresters,
        For farmers,
                We praise you.

For Christ's blessing of bread,
For revealing the divine presence in earthly things,
        We praise you.

The Arthur Rank Centre

Respect for the Earth

The earth and everything in it belong to the Lord (Psalm 24 : 1)

We thank you, Lord God,
for the life you have given to the world you created
and for the promise of new life

4

which you have given us
through your son Jesus Christ.

Christian Aid

Litany of Praise

Let the Earth praise God.
Praise Our Creator.
Praise the Source of Life, All Creation.
Praise Our Creator.
Sing praise to the Holy One for ever.
Praise Our Creator.
Skies above and waters below,
Praise Our Creator.
Sun, moon, stars and planets,
Praise Our Creator.
Rain and dew, winds and breezes,
Praise Our Creator.
Fire and heat, ice and cold,
Praise Our Creator.
Green plants and ancient forests,
Praise Our Creator.
Birds of the air and fish of the sea,
Praise Our Creator.
Nights and days, years and centuries,
Praise Our Creator.
Frost and snow, lightning and thunder,
Praise Our Creator.
Mountains and hills, lakes and rivers,
Praise Our Creator.
Winged, multi-legged, four-legged and two-legged creatures,
Praise Our Creator.

Diann Neu
USA

God in Creation

God's spirit dwells within all he has made,
The animals in forest, field and glade,
The birds that fly and soar across the sky,
The insects small, and fish in waters deep.

God's spirit dwells within all he has made,
He gave them form and life with his own breath,
To every creature whether large or small,
He saw them all and he pronounced them good.

God's spirit dwells within all he has made,
The flowers wild and in our gardens grown,
The grass in fields and crops which pastures yield,
The forest trees and those which bear good fruit.

God's spirit dwells within all he has made,
And that is what makes all things beautiful,
And if we view them with the eyes of God,
We see his grace beyond Man's suffering.

God's spirit dwells within all he has made,
Each second, minute, hour of every day,
Creation's elements of sight and sound,
Transparency, through which God's light is seen.

Tune: Woodlands

Ruth Norton

Creation

We praise you, our Creator,
for the grandeur and mystery of the universe.
Its stretching back in time
and its reaching out in space
are beyond our imagining.

We praise you, for the miracle of life on earth,
the mysterious creation of living beings,
the eternal cycle of life and death,
the countless emergence of new out of old.
We praise you, for the infinity of different creatures,
each unique in its own way,
each fitting into its own niche
and all dependent on one another.
We praise you, our Creator.

Alan Litherland

Spirit of Creation and Community

Let us give thanks to the Spirit
whose restless energy dances through all creation.
Spirit of creation and community
we celebrate your power.

Let us give thanks to the Spirit
whose tender embrace gives birth to our longing.
Spirit of creation and community
we celebrate your power.

Let us give thanks to the Spirit
whose urgent voice summons us to justice.
Spirit of creation and community
we celebrate your power.

Let us give thanks for the first-fruits of the earth
and rejoice in the Spirit who gives bread for our hunger.
Spirit of creation and community
we celebrate your power.

Let us give thanks for the cup of salvation
and rejoice in the Spirit who gives wine for our sharing.
Spirit of creation and community
we celebrate your power.

Let us give thanks for the food of today
as we long for the feasting of all creation.
**Spirit of creation and community
we celebrate your power**.

Jan Berry

A Gardener's Delight

Gardeners delight in the gift of God in the extravagance of the
fruitful earth. They see the loving skill of the creating God as
they watch the seasons shape and re-shape plants and trees.
They marvel that the earth which sifts through their hands
and gives way to their hoes holds seed in its darkness in
preparation for its release into light.

Gardeners see that it is good, don't they?

Gardeners delight in the gift of God in the extraordinary variety of plants and trees. They marvel at the way God has loved
each of these into life – gerberas and camellias, oranges and
persimmons, spinach and rosemary. They laugh that a weed
in one place is a cultivated flower in another.

You gardeners see that it is good, don't you?

Gardeners delight in the gift of God who placed the different
together – the smallest of bulbs growing in the comforting
shade of the largest of trees. The sharp yellow of marigolds
softened by the blue of forget-me-nots. They are amazed at the
colours of creation.

We gardeners see that it is good, don't we?

Gardeners delight that God made people in many shapes and
sizes, people of different colours and languages. Gardeners

know that we flourish when we are in touch with others, when we share ideas and understandings.

Don't we?

The Uniting Church in Australia

The Beauty of Your Handiwork

O God who has placed us within the interwoven fabric of nature, help us to appreciate the beauty of your handiwork. Enable us to discern your artist's hand and heart within the mountains and valleys, the rivers and the plains, the sea, the sky and all of the earth with the vast array of plant and animal life which it sustains.

William L. Wallace
Aotearoa New Zealand

Statement of Faith

We believe that God hopes and works for a world where
    all shall be included in the feast of life
and that in Christ we see how costly it is to bring that world
    about.

We believe that God's strategy for a new world is to put
    the poorest first
and that nothing is more important for God's people than
    to bring the poor good news.

We believe that rich and poor alike can be generous, wise
    and creative because all are made in God's image
and that all are made poorer when any are left out.

We confess that we use our strength to protect ourselves
   and order the world to benefit the rich and not the poor
and that none of us can be trusted with too much power over
   others.

We believe that loving our neighbours means working for
   justice
so that all have a say in what happens to them.

We believe that God made the earth to sustain and delight us
and that we are called to take care of it and enjoy it.

We believe that the God of all the earth is at work beyond
   the churches as well as within them
making common cause with all who want the poor to be
   included.

We long for the time when the meek shall inherit the earth
   and all who hunger and thirst after justice shall be satisfied
and we believe that, despite the persistence of evil, now is
   always the time when more good can be done and we can
   make a difference.

Christian Aid

Rivers, Mountains and Trees

Albuquerque dawn, like an icon of praise
To a God who paints pictures to lighten our days
Who dances on the morning and opens our eyes
A God who's an artist and who loves to surprise.

North Carolina in the time of fall
A carpet of leaves covers it all
Beautiful sunlight makes everything gold
Brings shimmers of glory to comfort your soul.

Chorus: The rivers, the mountains and the trees
            Wind off the desert, walks by the sea
            Gold leaves in the autumn and warm summer breeze.
            Like a holy touch of mercy that helps us to breathe,
            The rivers, the mountains and the trees.

Down at Port Alfred you can sit there all day
Watch the dolphins swim past somewhere around ten
Then in the evening they're back without fail
And, if you're lucky, you may see a whale.

Chorus: The rivers . . .

Passing Loch Lomond, heading up to Loch Ness
Passing Ben Nevis but the part I love best
Is the awe and fear as you go through Glencoe.
Such a strict God as the mountains loom close.

Chorus: The rivers . . .

There's a tale that is told from the Southern Sudan
About a tree where life began.
And it's strange how our myths and our stories agree
There's something quite special that begins with a tree.

Chorus: The rivers . . .

The hills of Jerusalem now disappear
Wrapped up in concrete and buried with tears.
Up north birds are singing on a mountain by the sea
It happens to be where a man talked of peace.

Chorus: The rivers . . .

Mystical moment – speak to me still
From the Church of St Francis next to Bray Hill.
Did I feel God breathing – did the earth really shake?
Centuries of prayer – all for our sake.

11

Chorus: The rivers . . .

Snapshots of beauty returning to me
Make me so grateful for all that I've seen.
Images so wild in the surf and the rain
O the power and the beauty from a strength that's not tame.

Chorus: The rivers . . .

Garth Hewitt

A Tree-Planting Liturgy

*This liturgy can be conducted at the time of a
tree-planting ceremony*

Look at the stagnant water
where all the trees were felled.
Without trees the water-holes mourn,
without trees the gullies form
for the tree roots that bind the soil are gone!
We plant these seedlings today as an admission of guilt.
Indeed there were forests and abundance of rain
but we left the land naked.
Like a person in shame
our country is shy in its nakedness.
Our tree planting today is a sign of harmony between us and
   creation.
We are reconciled with creation through Jesus' body and
   blood which brings peace.
He came to save all creation.

*At this point the sacramental bread and wine is served. Each
communicant holds a seedling in his/her hand while receiving the
sacrament and then proceeds to where the holes have been dug in
the new woodlot. Before the actual planting the bishop walks through
the woodlot, sprinkling holy water on the ground saying:*

This is the water of purification and fertility.
We sprinkle it on this new acre of trees.
It is a prayer to God, a symbol of rain
so that trees will grow and the land will heal.

Zionist Bishop Reuben Marinda

Peace Trees

To be in the presence of peace trees
Is to know peace.
The silent rhythm of their life,
Bringing maturity in due time,
Without anxiety or haste,
Calms our impatience;
Their solid strength, derived from
Hidden roots spreading much further
Than we ever know, gives us security;
Grace, beauty, shapeliness and form,
Delight our senses, soothe our
Fragile nerves, and bring refreshment.
Let us in turn be trees,
Growing in God's time to maturity,
Spreading our roots deep into springs of life,
Opening branches wide to all who come,
Offering strength and healing through our
Peace.

Ann Lewin

Coconut Tree

My stifled mind
gazes on your trunk
standing tall and gracious
bending and unbending
caressed and battered

by wind, people, other creatures
yet never accepting
to be broken down
nor torn apart
within yourself
of your own accord

May your own strength
be my own
May your wisdom
be my own

My broken heart
yearns for your fruits
The cosy clusters
round and solid
growing on the tree top
sweet and cool water
the inward spring spontaneous
shielded by self protective hardshell
to quench thirst
of people in toil
to survive under tropical heat
And your meat to nourish
the poor of south

Your shells are used
for creative images of art work
or to be offered for fuel

Your message is
to say 'No' to any waste
and 'Halt' to all wastefulness
of greed and domination

Oh, coconut tree
of the south
a being that is heart-warming
a presence revealing a truth
of God Universal
The eternal source of all life

Sun-Ai Lee Park
Malaysia

Celebrating the Uniqueness of Trees

Nothing of our coconut tree is ever lost. Its fibrous trunk is used for lumber. Its leaves are used for roofing of nipa houses, while the midribs of its leaves are made into broomsticks. Its fruits are delightful nourishment and its fresh juice, besides satisfying thirst, has a healing value for kidney ailments. Both fruit and juice are used in a variety of Filipino dishes. When only the husk remains, even this is made useful in the cleaning of wooden floors. The decorative arts find good material in its dry husk and leaves.

Coconut planters have their workers take great risks to climb high and gather the oil which is used in cooking as well as for wine-making and healthy hair.

Coconut groves beautify our seashores for they rise tall and strong. They weather any storm.

Let us celebrate the stately beauty and usefulness of our Coconut tree.

The young leaves and fruits of the Tamarind tree are used for souring certain Filipino dishes – the 'sinigang'. The ripe pods are eaten or made into syrups, beverages and candied sweets.

Let us celebrate these gifts of our Tamarind tree.

The Malunggay tree has tiny green leaves often used in Filipino dishes like 'tinolang manok'. Herbalists say it is very rich in iron and its seeds, when dried, may be eaten raw and can be used as a diuretic. The poultice of the leaves is used for laxative purposes and for glandular swellings.

Let us celebrate the rich medicinal properties of the Malunggay tree.

The Avocado seed can easily sprout and grow into a tree whose leaves are plucked for avocado tea. Its pear-shaped fruit is either green or violet brown. A single ripe fruit is commonly equated in nutritious value as equivalent to six eggs. It used to be a common, ordinary fruit, until its nourishing richness became known and appreciated.

Let us celebrate our friend the Avocado tree.

The Mango tree is a rich source of vitamin C. It produces luscious green fruits which turn yellow when ripe. Its leaves when boiled in water can bring cure for colds, or when dipped in hot water and applied externally can ease arthritic pains. The decoction of the leaves is antidiuretic. The oil of the seed is useful in chronic malarial fever. We find mango leaves in the now famous 'pito-pito' herbal tea (*pito* = seven leaves of tea).

Let us celebrate the rich medicinal properties of the Mango tree.

The Bamboo is noted for its beauty and elegance. It sways with the wind or creaks in heavy storms but it never breaks. Because of its hollow inside its usefulness is seen in irrigation of rice lands and other crops. The decorative arts, too, appreciate the bamboo. The symbolism of the bamboo swaying rather than breaking and its emptiness within speak louder than any book on spirituality could ever do.

Let us celebrate these life-giving qualities of the Bamboo.

The Narra, which is our Filipino national tree, is known for its hardness, usefulness and rapid growth, as well as for its adaptability to any kind of soil. It is a windfirm tree that can withstand strong storms. Its branches spread wide like a gigantic umbrella and provide shade and shelter to many creatures.

May these sturdy trees be a symbol of our steadfastness in faith and hope in Christ.
May we constantly anchor our life in Christ who is our all.

Pax Christi
The Philippines

You Who are in the Wind

Almighty God,
you who are in the wind
that breathes on the sea,
and the waves of the ocean;
the seal on the rocks;
the lark in the heavens;
the rays of the sun;
and the glittering rock in the valley;
you who are in the whole of creation
and in your loved ones,
we give you thanks and offer praise.

The Society of Our Lady of the Isles

Affirmation of Faith

We believe that creation is a gift of God,
an expression of our Creator's goodness.
We believe that as human beings we are part of this creation,
and that we share in a special way in the creative power of
God.

17

We believe that the resources of our land and waters and air
are precious gifts from our Creator,
to be used and looked after with loving care.
We believe that there is a rhythm to God's creation, like a
    drum beat;
when we lose the beat, or the drum is damaged, the music is
    out of tune.

The Pacific Women's Consultation
on Justice, Peace and the Integrity of Creation

Praise You Lord

We praise you Lord
for the wonders of life on our planet,
and we give you thanks
for all that the earth provides
for our food,
shelter and well-being.
We commit to you
those areas of the world
where the resources of nature have been plundered
and people's livelihoods threatened;
and we pray for those who work
to restore the land to people
who most need its harvest.

Christian Aid

Rainbow God

Rainbow God,
we praise you for the beauty of planet earth;
for the deep blue of the oceans
with the splendour of sea creatures,
shy shellfish hidden in crevices,
spouting whales majestically riding the waves,
playful dolphins trying new games

and vast shoals of multi-coloured fish;
for the variety of sea life,

We praise your name, good Lord.

For the green meadows and heather-covered hills,
for orchards abundantly producing apples, red and green,
for fields of barley, corn and yellow mustard,
for herds of cows, replete with milk,
for flocks of sheep, caring for playful lambs,
for horse chestnut brown, milk white and coal black;
for all the variety of the countryside

We praise your name, good Lord.

For the sun that shines bright in the sky,
for the clouds, pregnant with rain, showering blessings,
for scent-filled air, life-sustaining,
for the majestic eagle, soaring over mountains,
for the lark, filling the air with her song,
for lines of geese, heading for home;
Rainbow God, for all this loveliness

We praise your name and give you thanks.

John Johansen-Berg

Dreamer at Prayer

God of creation, Designer supreme
Our sensitive weaver of action or dream,
>   With praise we adore you; we feast on your gaze,
>   Endearing, unending, O radiance of days.

To God of the workplace, to God of all skills
We bring our thanksgiving, we offer our wills.
>   With you, and your colleagues, let's work with our hands
>   To love and to cherish; to pray for all lands.

19

God of all unions, all parties, all creeds
Bring us to new life through being, not deeds.
> In the name of the Godhead, the Spirit, the Son,
> As God's healing leads us, may all become one.

God of the Cosmos, great God beyond time,
When limits beset us, or sorrow or crime,
> Be close to support us; ordain us as thine;
> Through grace and through wholeness may forgiving
> light shine.

God of the landscape, dear God of all life,
May you, our provider, forgive us for strife.
> For those who face drought, and daily distress
> Let your Spirit guide us, the needy to bless.

Wendy Whitehead

Butterfly

The dance of the butterfly
Sings of joy,
Sings of beauty
And of peace,
Mirrors the wonder
Of the transformation in our lives.

Within a dark chrysalis
A life lies dormant,
In a dark chrysalis which is so small,
So insignificant,
So tiny in the hands of the Creator
As it hangs unnoticed and uncared for.

Yet,
Deep within, a caterpillar is dying,
Dying to self;

Changing
In the warmth of God's embrace.

Slowly, patiently, secretly
Being transformed
Until
In His own way and His own time
A new life
Is ready to be revealed.

And when the timing is Just Right
For the great Creator's plan,
The new life breaks free.
Beauty is revealed,
Created from the ordinariness of a dusty chrysalis.

Nervously at first,
Uncertain of the fragility of the newness which it feels.
Slowly, trustingly,
The wings of the butterfly
Open themselves fully
To the sunshine of God's love.
And as the healing rays of love
Strengthen those fragile wings
New confidence is born.

The butterfly takes off
In a dance of joyous celebration,
Radiantly reflecting back to the world
The beauty
And the love
Of God.

Pat Marsh

Awareness

Creator of heaven and earth,
from the nearest flower in the garden
to the farthest galaxy in the universe,
broaden our minds
to grasp the connectedness of all created things.

As our knowledge expands
to probe more and more into the secrets of life,
as our communications improve
to see at first hand what is happening far away,
help us the better to understand the links
between past and present
and between events and trends the world over.

Remind us that just as ocean currents in the Pacific
affect the weather over England
and chemicals we put into the air
affect the ozone layer over the Antarctic
so our lives are conditioned by events
in other countries and other cultures
and everything we do has reverberations for the rest of
    humankind.

Alan Litherland

The Jewel on the Cushion

A tiny jewel
Nestling on the fragrance of a soft pink cushion
Encapsulates a celebration
Of the wonder of the great creator's hand.

There is tenderness, beauty,
Joy, potential:
All these are framed within this minute snapshot
Of the wider panoramic world.

22

Tiny rainbows of colour
Reflecting and bouncing from the surface of the jewel
Dazzle the senses.

Deep in the softness
Of this little pink cushion,
There is expectation, potential,
New life waiting to be awakened,
Waiting to grow and blossom
Into something
Unimaginably more beautiful
And more radiant than before.

Within the father-heart of all mankind
There is potential
For hidden beauty
To be born.

Just as God's love
Transforms
The raindrop on the rosebud
Into precious jewel on velvet cushion,
So God's love
Can change us all.

Pat Marsh

St Francis

A Eucharistic Prayer

Father,
we praise you for your servant Francis,
who, bearing in his body the marks of Jesus;
learned to possess everything
without clinging to possessions,

and, by embracing the leper
taught us that what is not lovely in us
is loved and healed by your grace.

Rejoicing like him in your great love
in creation, we join all your creatures
in heaven and earth, and praise you
saying (singing)
Holy, holy, holy Lord,
God of joy and life;
Heaven and earth are full of your glory,
Hosanna in the highest.

Hear us now, as we meet to remember Jesus,
who on the night before he died,
took bread and wine,
blessed them
and gave them to his friends, saying
This is my body, this is my blood,
given for you.

Come freshly to us now, Lord God,
and fill us with your Spirit;
that we may be surprised into
new discoveries of the simplicity
and generosity of your love, through Jesus Christ our Lord,
Amen

Ann Lewin

As Keen as Mustard

A meditation for children

I am a small seed—
in actual fact, the smallest.
Deep beneath the earth
is where I now lie.

But if I want to live,
then, first I must die.

Letting go of me
will be the hardest task.
But when that is done,
I'll make a new start.
I'll grow strong, wide and high,
with shade beneath my boughs
for those who pass by.

I'll keep a look-out
for things I can do,
that will be of service
to each one of you.

My very proudest moment
was when Jesus told you:
'With mustard-seed-sized faith,
there's nothing you can't do.'

Susan Hardwick

The Seed

Deep within the dark and cold of earth,
Beneath the ground brown plough
And the tail end
Of fickle springtime's chilling rains,
There winds a thread
In secret silence hidden.

Unbidden it comes
In sweet time all its own,
And with a strength by fragile form belied
It penetrates the soil from deep within,

And works both up and down
To form the anchor and the mast
Of next year's bread.

The sun climbs soon, and warmly smiles
To see the silent early greening
Mist enclothe the land—
Veiled as a mother's breast
With modest rich potential.

Spring gains to summer's heat,
With swallows weaving high above the corn,
And far beyond belief and sight
The lark rejoices endlessly
At Heaven's door . . .
Whilst on the floor of earth
The sheathed leaves grow and ripen to fruition
Whispering their secrets in the idle winds—
Until at last the gold is set
And stands in glowing richness in the fields,
Tall, strong, and laden with the bursting seed
In readiness for harvest
And the gathering of gifts . . .

And endless thankfulness.

Still later, in the autumn mists
And wreaths of coming cool,
When trees relinquish green to gold
And fall to nakedness—
Then will the plough return
The stubbled earth to rest,
And in the breathlessness of winter's sleep
It waits in silence for the hidden spring . . .

And seed time's infinitely sweet return.

Margot Arthurton

God of the Whirlwind

Based on Job 38:1–18

God of the whirlwind,
we realise we were not there.
You made it all without us,
from the earth's foundations
to the highest heavens.
You alone shut the doors of the sea
and made, from the clouds,
a coat for the earth.
We confess that sometimes we act
as if we did it all,
as if we have all the answers.
We confess that we tear the blanket of mystery
that protects your fragile creation
and try to make it look as if
we understand everything.
Forgive us.
We would seek your kingdom,
respect the earth,
honour one another
and build communities of hope.

Janet Lees

Praise God for Things that Grow

Crocus pushing through the earth,
      Tadpole turning into frog,
Chicken tapping at the shell,
      Baby kicking in the pram.

      Praise God for things that grow:
      Praise God for things that grow.

Ladybird with fragile wings,
      Seagull wheeling overhead,
Kite that tugs the slender cord,
      Pilot coming into land.

      Praise God for things that fly:
      Praise God for things that fly.

Sun and moon and starry sky,
      Crystal snowflakes drifting down,
Pavements wet with summer rain,
      Coloured lights at Christmas time.

      Praise God for things that shine:
      Praise God for things that shine.

Blackbird opening wide his beak,
      Wind and wave and waterfall,
Engine humming, clanging bell,
      All our voices raised in song.

      Praise God for things that sing:
      Praise God for things that sing.

Elizabeth Cosnett

Painted Flowers

O, thank the Lord, for the whiteness of the snowdrop,
   and for the carpet of the yellow dancing daffodil.
For the painted colours of the tulip,
   and the shades of brown of the wallflower.

O, thank the Lord, for the wooded bluebell dells,
   and the pink and white of blossoms on the trees.
For the painted colours of the forget-me-not,
   and the dainty face of the pansy.

28

O, thank the Lord, for fragrant honeysuckle,
    and the rambling cottage rose.
For the painted colours of the foxglove,
    and the rainbow shades of sweet pea.

O, thank the Lord, for the boldness of the dahlia,
    and the fiery colours of the geranium.
For the painted colours of the fuchsia,
    and the grandeur of the gladioli.

Frances Ballantyne

Harvest People

Blessed are those who trust in the Lord,
    who acknowledge Jesus as God's Son.
They will be like a tree planted by the water,
    full of nourishment, vitality and strength.
Sending out its roots by the stream,
    growing effectively with nourishment,
it does not fear when heat comes,
    nothing causes them to become discouraged.
Its leaves are always green,
    deeds of kindness are always apparent.
It has no worries in a year of drought,
    utter confidence in God's provision
and never fails to bear fruit,
    harvest yield is always excellent.

Frances Ballantyne

Take a Look!

Voice One: Look! At the flowers in the gardens.
Voice Two: We did and we saw your beauty.
Voice One: Look! At the birds of the air.
Voice Two: We did and we saw your freedom.

Voice One:	Look! At the grass of the moorland.
Voice Two:	We did and we saw your endurance.
Voice One:	Look! At the fish of the oceans.
Voice Two:	We did and we saw you in diversity.
Voice One:	Look! At the trees in the woods.
Voice Two:	We did and we saw your steadfastness.
Voice One:	Look! At the sand on the seashore.
Voice Two:	We did and we saw your abundance.
Voice One:	Look! At the snow on the mountainside,
Voice Two:	We did and we saw your grandeur.
Voice One:	Look! At the harvest in the fields.
Voice Two:	We did and we saw your provision.
Voice One:	Look at the world, it's my creation.
Voice Two:	We did and we saw your handiwork
Voice One:	Look! Take a look! At a cross on the hillside.
Voice Two:	We did and we saw such love.

Frances Ballantyne

We Belong to the Earth

During these Opening Responses flowers, fruits, vegetables, water, lights may be brought in from all four corners of the place of worship and put on and around the altar. *A harvest or creation hymn may be sung at any point.*

Calls to worship based on Psalm 104:

Leader: Bless the Lord, O my soul, O Lord, my God,
you are very great. You are clothed with honour
and majesty, wrapped in light as with a garment.

All: **Come praise the Lord**.

Leader: You stretch out the heavens like a tent,
you set the beams of your chambers on the waters.
You set the earth on its foundations,
so that it shall never be shaken.

All: **Come praise the Lord**.

Leader: You make springs gush forth in the valleys;
they flow between the hills,
giving drink to every wild animal.

All: **Come praise the Lord**.

Leader: You cause the grass to grow for the cattle,
and plants for people to use,
to bring forth food from the earth,
and wine to gladden the human heart.

All: **Come praise the Lord**.

Leader: May the glory of the Lord endure for ever;
may the Lord rejoice in His works.

All: **Come praise the Lord**.

*Two further variations of Psalm 104, one from the Pacific region
and one from Africa:*

Praise of Creation from Melanesia

Leader: For the earth and all its parts:
All: **We praise you, O God**.

Leader: For the cliffs, which show forth your strength,
and your unchanging, never-ending love:
All: **We praise you, O God**.

Leader: For the shells, which show forth your variety
and your joy in creating the world,
which you have entrusted to our care:
All: **We praise you, O God**.

31

Leader: For coconuts and taro plants,
which show forth your care for us:

All: **We praise you, O God.**

Leader: For the birds, which show forth our freedom
as your children:

All: **We praise you, O God.**

Leader: For the fish in the sea,
and the land animals,
which remind us of the new earth,
where your people live in peace,
working and sharing together:

All: **We praise you, O God.**

Leader: For the variety, spontaneity
and growth of insects,
which show forth death and resurrection
to new life,
the central message of your Son,
Jesus Christ, to us:

All: **We praise you, O God.**

Leader: For resemblances between people,
Which show forth your desire
that there might be one flock,
and one Shepherd:

All: **We praise you, O God.**

Leader: For differences between people,
such as are found in our islands
in the various languages,
traditions, customs and denominations,
which bring out the challenge of your word
and your message to each one of us:

All: **We praise you, O God.**

Leader: For all who are present at this celebration,
who through their commitment,
their willingness to hear and learn,
the openness of their hearts and minds,
show forth your readiness to forgive our sins
against you:

All: **We praise you, O God.**

Praise of Creation from Africa

Leader: Rejoice in the Lord,
for he has refreshed the parched earth.
Where there was nothing but brown,
hard, dead land,
now the soft earth is covered with fresh green.
Where death was in power,
new life has come forth,
awakening hope throughout the land.

All: **We praise you, O God.**

Leader: For the clouds which protect us from the sun,
for the thunder,
at which the earth trembles,
for the lightning which splits the sky:

All: **We praise you, O God.**

Leader: Rejoice for the rain that falls by night,
and soaks at once into the dry ground,
causing half-dried-up roots to swell,
and the deep cracks in the earth to close.
Rejoice for the cool nights,
the budding flowers,
the shooting trees,
and the tender, green grass:

All: **We praise you, O God.**

Leader: Rejoice for the great drops that fall at midday;
rejoice for the small streams,
singing on their way
from the hills down into the valleys,
to make the rivers swell
and fill the reservoirs,
and supply the cities
and irrigation channels with water:

All: **We praise you, O God**.

Leader: Rejoice over the new activity in the villages,
where housewives take their hoes and baskets
and hurry to the fields,
to test the fruitfulness of the earth
by planting seeds of hope and expectation.
Rejoice for those who have already
prepared their seedbeds,
and are now hurrying to try the strength
of carefully chosen seeds:

All: **We praise you, O God**.

Leader: For the ground,
for rain, for seeds and tools,
for strength in arms and backs,
for the will to work
and for creative minds:

All: **We praise you, O God**.

Thanksgiving

Leader: Every part of this earth is sacred.
Whatever befalls the earth befalls the children of
the earth.
This we know, the earth does not belong to us:

All: **We belong to the earth**.

Leader: This we know, all things are connected:

All: **Like the blood which unites one family**.

Leader: This we know, we did not weave the web of life:
All: **We are merely a thread in it**.

Leader: This we know, whatever we do to the web:
All: **We do to ourselves**.

Benediction

Leader: As we prepare to leave and embrace the challenges
        of our lives and our world,
        let us ask for God's blessing.
        May God bless us with strength to seek justice,
All: **Amen**.
Leader: May God bless us with wisdom to care for our
        earth.
All: **Amen**.
Leader: May God bless us with love to bring forth new life.
All: **Amen**.
Leader: In the name of God, the maker of the whole world,
        of Jesus, our new covenant,
        and of the Holy Spirit,
        who opens our eyes and hearts.
All: **Amen**.
Leader: Go in peace and be witnesses to hope.
All: **Thanks be to God**.

Sinfonia Oecumenica
Germany

Part Two:
Sharing in God's work

'The Lord God took the man and put him
in the Garden of Eden to work it and
take care of it.'
Genesis 2:15

Creator God

Creator God,
you gave us paradise,
an earth producing abundance
in fields and orchards, lakes and oceans.
We have not been good stewards
of such precious gifts.
We have polluted the seas with impurities;
we have desecrated the earth with poisons;
we have ruined the air with radiation.
Forgive us for our betrayal of mother earth;
help us to take better care
of the planet which is our inheritance.

Loving God,
we give thanks that we belong to the land
and are one with your creation.
The land is precious
and has sustained our family through generations.
The land gives us birth
when we begin our journey of earthly life;
the land receives us back
when we complete the journey in death.
We find in the land
our place of celebration.
We make our home in the land
and it meets our daily needs.
Living God,
we give you thanks for your precious gift of the land.

God of abundant harvest,
help us to recognize and maintain
the balance of nature for the common good.
Let us not exhaust the earth
by constant sowing and reaping, without rest for the
    fields;
let us not expect more from the earth
than we are prepared to give to it.
As the land blesses us with its produce
so may we enrich it with water and with minerals.
God of goodness,
inspire us to give and to receive
in our relationship with mother earth.

Good Lord, forgive us.
You have placed into our care
the variety of animals, tame and wild.
We have not cared for them as we should;
we have hunted and destroyed;
we have eliminated whole species.
Elephants are slaughtered for ivory;
leopards are killed to provide a coat or dress;
stags are hunted and killed for drawing-room decoration
and tigers become a rich man's rugs.
Forgive us that we think so highly of ourselves
and treat other animals with such disdain.
You did not place creation in our care
to be so misused and hurt.
Forgive us and help us
to show compassion to the creatures of land and sea.

John Johansen-Berg

Co-Creators of the Earth

God, you have made us co-creators of the earth.
You have entrusted us with all the resources of the world to
    care for and share.

Help us always to be gentle with our planet.
Help us not to pollute the atmosphere or the waterways.
Help us not to waste precious resources like energy or food.
Help us always to be aware of the effects modern technology
   may have on the environment.

Christian Aid and CAFOD

Prayer in the Vegetable Garden

O God, Creator and Source of Life,
we thank you for the gifts
given from your abundance
and through the work of human hands
by which we are blessed with nourishing food.
Pour your blessings on this garden
and on all that grows within it,
and on those who toil in it with love and reverence,
that the earth may yield its abundance
and we and all your children may be fed.
Through Jesus Christ our Lord.
Amen

Community of the Sisters of the Church

Tenderness between People

Voice One: Let us pray for tenderness between people, in
communities:
where economic activity is based on
   greed,
where only the wealthy and ambitious are
   respected,
where the poorest and weakest go unseen,
and each one feels alone, especially . . .
(name people known to you)

And we give thanks for communities:
>   where the silent have found their voice,
>   where the unseen work of many is
>   affirmed with pride:
>   where those who were treated as nothing
>   have discovered that they matter,
>   and they are not alone, especially . . .
>   *(name people known to you)*

For the foolishness of God is wiser than our
wisdom.

All: **And the weakness of God is stronger than our strength**.

Voice Two: Let us pray for tenderness within the law, in communities:
>   where the poorest have no share in the
>   land,
>   where conditions of work are degrading
>   and divisive,
>   where a few determine the lives of many
>   and the voice of protest is silent,
>   especially . . .
>   *(name situations known to you)*

And we give thanks for communities:
>   where the poor have pooled resources to
>   support each other,
>   where those with knowledge have used it
>   to help others learn,
>   where the interests of the strongest have
>   been challenged
>   with anger and courage and love,
>   especially . . .
>   *(name situations known to you)*

42

For the foolishness of God is wiser than our wisdom.

All: **And the weakness of God is stronger than our strength**.

Voice Three: Let us pray for tenderness between the earth and its people, in a world community:
> where crops are grown not to feed children but for foreign debt,
> where forests are destroyed that help the earth to breathe,
> where fertile land is exhausted and air and water sickened with pollution, especially . . .
> *(name places known to you)*

And we give thanks for communities:
> where land is more fairly shared,
> where the forest is both harvested and sustained,
> where desert has been reclaimed and clean water brings life and health, especially . . .
> *(name places known to you)*

For the foolishness of God is wiser than our wisdom.

All: **And the weakness of God is stronger than our strength.**

Christian Aid

Asebech's Family

Nine-year-old Asebech lives with her parents and two brothers in the highlands of Ethiopia about 250 kilometres north of the capital, Addis Ababa.

Asebech's extended family forms a small community of four households called Zergaw's Water. The combined effect of droughts and civil war have made this region one of the poorest in the country. The soil is almost barren and the bitter fighting of the war destroyed roads, transport and market systems as well as sending the inhabitants, including Asebech's family, into hiding.

Now, they have returned to their homes to pick up their lives again. The development wing of the Ethiopian Orthodox Church (EOC) has been working with the people of the region since the end of the war. It has covered the village spring with a concrete slab to protect it from pollution by animals and the water runs into a tank to keep it clean. People get their water from a tap while the animals drink from a pool below.

A clinic providing basic health care has been opened near the village and to improve the health of the community even further some of the farmers have been given seeds and tools. Asebech's grandfather, Kelem Belete, is one of the farmers who has received help. His story is on page 197. He now grows apples, carrots, cabbage, lettuce and beetroot. He has never seen these fruits and vegetables before but he is learning how to grow them and is introducing them to his neighbours.

Asebech's family has two cows and a calf, an ox and three sheep. They grow their own food, selling any surplus in the market to earn cash for clothes, exercise books or other needs. But the soil is very poor. Before the involvement with the Ethiopian Orthodox Church, the family was struggling to produce enough to eat. Even now, their lifestyle is very basic.

The village tree nursery is another EOC venture. It employs thirty-one people who take turns to work, thus sharing out the opportunity and earnings it provides. Asebech's parents are part of this workforce which produces young trees for planting throughout the district. The aim of this programme is to improve the soil and limit erosion; its vision, that once more the hills of Ethiopia will be covered in trees and the country will be a productive and beautiful place to live in.

Christian Aid

Prayer in the Orchard, Bible and Prayer Gardens

O God, may your stillness and peace
rest upon our garden and orchard
and upon all who come to it.
May your presence permeate it,
your blessing be upon this place
and on those who tend it with love and reverence.
May fruit and flowers be brought forth in abundance
in our garden and within the garden of our hearts.
Through Jesus Christ our Lord.
Amen

Community of the Sisters of the Church

Prayer by the Rose Arbour

O God, source of all beauty,
we thank you for your presence in creativity
and for the beauty by which we are surrounded,
for colours and scents,
sounds and shapes,
delicacies and delights.
Pour your blessing on our garden–
on plants, flowers, trees, birds, animals, bees,
and on all who come here,
that its beauty may be a source of
healing, solace and joy.

Through Jesus Christ our Lord
who lives and reigns with you,
Creator God and the life-giving Spirit,
now and eternally.
Amen

Community of the Sisters of the Church

People Who Create

Living God, Creator of the World,
we pray for people who create,
in studios and on production lines,
sitting by computer screens and
working the soil,
people who are making things,
growing things:
we thank you for them,
we praise you for their work,
we ask you to bless them.

Living God, Saviour of the Word,
who came not to be served,
but to serve,
we pray for the people who serve,
who wait at table, who sweat in
fast food outlets,
who bathe elderly people,
who are constantly
answering phone queries:
we thank you for them,
we praise you for their work,
we ask you to bless them.

Living God, Giver of Life and Energy,
we pray for people whose work
helps us to work,
for chaplains and managers and
teachers and
personnel people, for
stewards of human resources,
and for those people in every walk of life
who inspire and
surprise and change
us:
we thank you for them,
we praise you for their work,
we ask you to bless them.

Bob Warwicker

The Earth is Our Mother

Teach your children what we have taught our children;
that the earth is our mother.
This we know;
the earth does not belong to humanity;
humanity belongs to the earth.
This we know.
All things are connected like the blood
that unites one family.
Whatever befalls the earth befalls
the sons and daughters of the earth.
Men and women did not weave the web of life:
they are merely a strand in it.
Whatever they do to the web,
they do to themselves.

Chief Seattle to the President of the United States, 1854
Christian Aid and CAFOD

The Earth is the Lord's

Based on Psalm 24

Hey man! Everything belongs to God.
And don't you dare to go around abusing it.
For you are responsible and accountable
for all that has been created.

Hey man! You are expected to live right
with all that has been created.
That means, being sensible and responsible
in everything you do.

Hey man! Rejoice and be happy in the
fellowship with God Almighty!

Youth in Mission Workcamp
Nauru, Central Pacific

The Care of the Earth

Creator God, breathing your own life into our being, you give
us the gift of life. You placed us on this earth with its flowers
and fruits, minerals and waters, living creatures of grace and
beauty. At harvest time the earth reaches the peak of its fruitfulness. It depends on us to praise you by harvesting its goods
in ways which ensure there will be harvests in the future.

You gave us the care of the earth.

Today you ask us: 'Where are you? What have you done?'

Silence may follow

Christian Ecology Link

Creative Carelessness

They cannot take away your sky, Lord,
though they try–
with their toxic gas emissions
and their CFC pollutions
and their smog-creating smoke clouds.
It's still there.
Blue and black
in day and night-time.
Sun and moon and stars that glisten,
clouds that glow and glower and rumble.
Sunset flare and sunrise glory
ever changing
yet eternal.
Yours, Lord.
How dare we ignore it
as if nothing we could do will permanently harm it?

Make us aware of our responsibilities.

They cannot take away your earth, Lord,
or its worth.
With their underground nuclear testing
and their careless deforestation.
It's still there.
Rainbow coloured
plants and animals,
trees and fruit and birds and fishes,
grass and grain and sparkling water,
land and sea and soaring mountain–
your provisions
for your children.
Yours, Lord.
How dare we misuse it
as if we need do nothing to protect it?

Make us aware of our stewardship.

Please, Lord,
before it's too late.

Marjorie Dobson

Prayer for Forgiveness

When we are unkind to people,
     and forget they are God's children,
When we are careless with the beasts
     and forget they are God's creation,
When we ill-treat the land,
     and forget it is the splendour of God,
Forgive us, O God of love, and reconcile us to yourself,
     to one another and to the Creation.
Teach us, that the earth and all its fullness is yours,
     the world and those who dwell in it.
Remind us that your Son too
     enjoyed the fruits of harvest in Galilee
     and joins us now as we celebrate your good gifts
      together.
Call us yet again to safeguard the gift of life,
     now and for ever.
Amen

Christian Ecology Link

Partners Together

When you ask us for commitment, Generous God,
let us remember the labour of six days for a just and fruitful
    earth;
the labour of three days for the reconciliation of a whole race;
the renewal of every day's labour by your life-giving breath;
and may this release in us

the generous response of shared hope,
that makes us partners together in the enterprise of life.

Janet Lees

Tools for Self-Reliance

For the harvesting of anvils
rusting in barns
Creator God we thank you.

For the singing of sewing machines
put to new use
Creator God we thank you.

For bobbins and pins
given new life
Creator God we thank you.

For buckets and pails,
for spanners and hammers,
for forks and for spades
rescued from dusty sheds,
Creator God we thank you.

For the harvest of tools, skills and hope
Bountiful God we thank you.

For those who give
and those who refurbish
tools for self-reliance;
for those who will receive and use
the harvest not of our fields
but of our past,
Lord of history we thank you.

Kate McIlhagga

Generosity

What should I give to the land?
Perhaps some return of the abundance I receive.
The land blesses me with grain, bread of life;
the sky blesses me with rain, water of life.
The land gives me abundant fruit, food of life;
the air gives me oxygen to breathe, spirit of life.
How can I number the blessings of earth?
It daily grants me gifts beyond counting.
The generosity of mother earth surpasses our expectation.
What then shall I give to the land?
Surely nothing less than the best stewardship
that I can offer through all the talents I possess.

John Johansen-Berg

Heavenly Artist

Heavenly Artist,
we thank you for the varied talents
of your great family, the human race;
for the great Russian composers,
for the majestic organ music of Germany,
for the plaintive violin of Romania,
for the joyful drums of Kenya,
for the temple bells of India
and the noisy bagpipes of Scotland.
For the music and the harmony of all the nations,
we give you thanks, good Lord.

John Johansen-Berg

Divine Embroiderer

Divine Embroiderer,
your people praise you in the rare beauty
of varied arts and crafts;

in the landscape painting of England,
the skilled wood carving of Zimbabwe,
the beautiful embroideries of Hungary,
the delicate lace of Spain and Ireland,
the miniature gardens of Japan,
and the stone carvings of India.
All these skills and crafted loveliness
praise your glorious name.

John Johansen-Berg

The Angel of the North

A meditation and prayer

The Angel stands, vast wings outstretched; geometrically –
unnaturally – straight wings, mimicking the horizontal rays of
an early morning sun which is bringing warmth and colour to
their dull, reddish brown surfaces. Rusty the Angel. An industrial angel for an industrial landscape. A sightless head gazing
out over chemical works, engineering plants, marshalling
yards.

At his feet the traffic hurries by. White blurs of faces at the
windows:

'Oh look. There it is.'

'Isn't it big?'

But the racing vehicles don't stop to contemplate the Angel
on his artificial hill overlooking the artificial landscape.
They've got to get to where they're going. There's no time.
And they leave him there, erect, immobile. Awaiting the
millennium.

With, at his stiffly braced back, sheltering behind those outstretched wings, the city. Rows of small identical boxes climbing the undulating fellside. And in the valley, beside the caged
and almost forgotten river, more boxes, huge boxes, the retail
park, the business park, the industrial park.

Yet this valley was once full of green growing things. If the

Angel could but turn his head there's still a memory, a concentrated vista of green farmland and small villages, church towers and copses, and away in the far distance the misty outline of the high moors.

But the Angel doesn't concern himself with what was. To an Angel what does the work of a couple of human generations matter? He concerns himself with what is and looks forward to what shall be.

Lord, give us the wisdom to do likewise. May we not long for some imagined, misty, long-ago golden age. May we not look back to some rustic never-never land. Give us the strength to deal with this world as it is and the determination to change it for the better. The small, identical boxes of the city may not be pretty, but we know that they're warm and comfortable, an immeasurable improvement on the pitmen's hovels that, 200 years ago, looked down on the same village church in the valley. The graceless and ugly industrial plant and offices may not be as romantic as the farmyards and byres they replaced, but they provide wealth and security at a level the farm labourers never knew. The immense, rusting Angel may not have the fragile beauty and grace of a Victorian Sunday School poster but he has his feet planted deep in the bones of this landscape. He's at one with this landscape. This working, changing landscape.

And it is changing: already at his feet where the pit-heap used to be the saplings that one day will form a new forest are bursting into life, while in the valley the gulls wheel and squabble over the rubbish being tipped to fill the scar of the old brickworks.

Lord, guide us to use the knowledge we've acquired to help repair the wounds we've inflicted on this world, your world, so that we can pass it on whole and beautiful to the generations who will be watched over by the Angel in years to come.

When we build remind us that it's for ourselves and for our posterity we're building, so that we give weight to aesthetics as well as to economics in the construction.

When we use the land remind us that it's a living thing, not a dead resource; as its stewards we must care for it and keep it in good health.

When we trade remind us that those with whom we trade are our brothers and sisters, entitled to their fair share of the bounty people wrest from your creation with the intellect you have gifted to us.

When as a nation we plan our finances, give us the wit to so design them that we can use the skills of all our people who wish to work, so that through our collective gifts we may remove drudgery and want from our society.

Finally, may we remember that you made us to be only a little lower than the Angels, however we think of them, rusty or glorious. Help us to aspire to be worthy of your design and craftsmanship, true children of our Creator, the Father of both humanity and of angels.

Amen

Alan Bell

The Farming Community

Hear us, O Lord, as we remember before you all in the
    farming community,
or whose lives are bound up in it, who have special need of
    you at this time:
all who fear for the continuation of their livelihood or
    employment;
all who must bear the loss of years of anxious toil
and the suffering of creatures entrusted to their charge;
all in doubt about the future for themselves and their families
and who feel themselves isolated and alone.
Uplift those that are cast down, O Lord, and cheer with hope
    all the discouraged:
uphold their faith, raise up helpers in their need
and grant that they may ever find peace, healing and hope.
Through Jesus Christ our Lord,
Amen

The Arthur Rank Centre

This Time of Crisis and Anxiety

God of the heavens and the earth,
You call us to share in the care of creation
and to bring food and fruitfulness from field and farm.
Hear our prayer for all who
make their living on the land
in this time of crisis and anxiety.

The Arthur Rank Centre

Times of Distress in the Farming Community

Creator God,
in times of uncertainty and fear,
help us to be aware of those who really care for us as people--
our families and friends and many others!

As we search for answers to our dilemmas,
grant a spirit of co-operation and trust.
To the officials and administrators give genuine sensitivity
    and wisdom,
to act swiftly and with compassion to those most needy.

As we unravel the mistakes may we learn the lessons, whatever they may be.
Above all as we seek to support each other through this time
may we simply rediscover how precious is our dependence
    on each other.
Amen

The Arthur Rank Centre

Our Ancestors Taught Us to Share

Our ancestors taught us to share
What we gather in a day.
We must keep the forest as the home of the animals
but also for pure water and air.

The only reason it still exists
is that we have taken care that it's not destroyed.
We need the forests for thatch,
for medicines and because they provide fruit.
The forest is our home.

Shipibo Indians, Peru
Christian Aid and CAFOD

In Times of Crisis

Eternal God, Creator and Sustainer of Life,
we praise you for the beauty and fertility of the earth.
We praise you also for its complexity and mystery
        before which we bow in wonder and awe.

Hear our prayers for all upon whom we depend
        for the production and provision of our food,
        for the management of the countryside and the
            husbanding of its resources.

To those who are suffering in a time of crisis bring comfort
    and hope,
to those entrusted with decision-making that affects others'
    lives
        give wisdom and discernment;
to your Church in its ministry to all,
        grant a watchful eye,
        a loving heart and
        a prophetic voice in the service of your kingdom.
Through Jesus Christ our Lord.
Amen

The Arthur Rank Centre

Part Three:

'Cursed is the ground . . .'

'By the sweat of your brow
you will eat your food.'

Genesis 2 : 19

Globalization

Your parent's heart grieves, good Lord,
whenever we cause suffering.
We have inherited a world of beauty
in which there is so much of good to share.
We have allowed the profit motive
to override the needs of the poor.
Where there is so much local talent
and parents work hard to sustain a family,
we have allowed the greed of multinational corporations
to blight the hopes of the poor.
When the richer nations claim monopoly of technology
and take advantage of the vulnerable,
primary producers suffer poverty and disease.
Inspire us, heavenly Friend, to change the system
so that each local community
is fairly rewarded for its skill and labour
and we become a global family where each cares for all.

John Johansen-Berg

Rice or Pineapples?

Bert and Nanette, who owned a small farm in the Philippines, needed to grow rice for the family's daily food. However, they were forced to grow pineapples instead. The fruit did not belong to them. They were not rich people but they were growing enough rice for their family to live on.

One day their daughter Ellie, aged ten, became ill with appendicitis. She needed an operation which cost money so Bert and Nanette sold their one water buffalo to pay for it.

Ellie got better but life for the family got a lot worse. They had used the buffalo to plough and do other jobs on the farm. In fact, they couldn't manage without it.

Just at the time they were caught up in this terrible situation, a pineapple company came along and offered to rent the farm from them for ten years. The company would give them 3,000 pesos a year and pay the first five years' rent immediately. Fifteen thousand pesos was more money than they had ever imagined. There was the possibility of work for Bert. They accepted the offer and the land that had grown their daily food was planted with pineapples to be sold to other countries.

Things turned out very badly. Bert's work lasted only six months of each year and with rising prices the money they had been given did not last long. Then Bert became sick from the pesticides he had to spray on the pineapples and so he wasn't able to work.

After ten years, Bert and Nanette thought they would get back their land. It was with a shock that they found they would have to pay for all the improvements the company had made to it – the roads, irrigation and electricity supply. The family couldn't afford it. The only thing to do was to move to the city and try to make a living on the streets.

Christian Aid

Peaceful Farmers

The Mapalad farmers of Sumilao in the Philippines have used peaceful means to gain access to land which was legally awarded to them by the Filipino government in 1995. They have been trying to obtain the legal paperwork for access to the 144 hectares but they were thwarted by the landowners who formerly owned the land. Despite violent opposition their campaign included land occupations, hunger strikes and flower petitions. Their harvest, in the meantime, was making and selling brooms by the roadside so that they could earn a living for their families and themselves.

Christian Aid

Cashew Crisis

In the 1950s Mozambique produced 50,000 tonnes of cashew nuts each year. In 1973 production peaked at 246,000 tonnes making Mozambique the world's biggest producer, growing enough nuts to keep fourteen factories going. In 1992 after the Mozambique war ended, privatization and liberalization came to dominate the economic policy of the Frelimo government. The cashew processing industry was one of the first casualties. On the advice of the World Bank, the unshelled nuts began to be exported for processing and the factories were closed.

Five thousand women lost their jobs in the Mozambique cashew nut industry. Bishop Mandalate questioned the wisdom of the World Bank's economic prescription to export nuts for processing rather than maintaining the domestic production process. When the last cashew nut factory closed, Fernando Faria de Castro, who managed the factory just outside the capital city of Maputo, said, 'I loved this place and the cashews we produced were the best quality. The factory stayed open even during the war but now it's gone, all gone.'

Christian Aid

The Importance of Clean Drinking Water

Karimun Nesa had been drinking contaminated water from a tube-well for 'a long time' before the Christian Commission for Development in Bangladesh (CCDB) disabled it. The scars on her hands show that the water she had been drinking contained dangerous levels of arsenic but at the time she had no idea why the scars were appearing.

In the 1960s a huge programme to install tube-wells in Bangladesh had lowered the incidence there of water-borne disease and child mortality but had inadvertently paved the way for another crisis.

Many of the tube-wells tapped water that was contaminated with naturally occurring arsenic at levels reaching 100 times the World Health Organization recommended limit. As many as 85 million people out of Bangladesh's population of 125 million may have been exposed to this contamination. While there is no cure for arsenic poisoning, if sufferers are prevented from drinking contaminated water, survival chances are high. CCDB will be testing half a million wells during the next three years, at a cost of £12 for 70 wells, and they are also identifying and marking accessible, alternative, safe sources of water, such as 'dug wells'. Until this is done, however, they can only encourage those whose drinking water is suspect to take preventative health measures, such as changing their diet to lower the risks from arsenicosis.

Fortunately for Karimun's daughter, Asha, CCDB disabled the well in her village just in time. She shows no signs of the skin blemishes, caused by arsenic poisoning, that could so easily have blighted her life.

Commitment for Life

Our Need for Water

Tesfai lives in a rural part of Ethiopia, in east Africa. At last it has begun to rain. It hasn't rained for a long time. He hopes that it will pour from the sky for days and days and soak into the dry ground. Then the animals will have a long drink and the crops will grow.

Mariam is a young girl who lives in Mali, west Africa. All the people in the village are very excited. A new well has been dug in the centre of the village. They used to walk for two hours to collect water, carrying it in a bucket on their heads. It was hard work. Now, they only have to walk for about five minutes.

Ranjit lives in a village in a rural part of south India in the state of Karnataka, 75 kms from the nearest town and 500 kms from Bangalore, the state capital. There has been no rain for two years. The district where he lives is registered as a drought-prone area which means that it is one of the poorest districts in India. The crops have failed on many occasions. The villages need bore wells.

Christian Aid
Geoffrey Duncan

Acute Shortages

Intermittent rainfall over three years, coupled with lengthy dry spells, has affected crop production and led to drought-induced acute food and water shortages for 1.3 million people in Northern Dafur, Sudan.

The Sudan Development Advisor of the Intermediate Technology Development Group, Mohammed Salih Farah, explains:

In the first few months of 2001 grain prices doubled due to diminishing stocks and low supplies, while livestock prices have currently dropped to only 30 per cent of what they were during the same period last year. In March 2001 goat owners had to sell three times the number of goats they would have sold in March 2000 to buy the same amount of millet. Women, who are responsible for over 80 per cent of agricultural activities and household subsistence, were having to walk long distances in search of the scarce food and water available for their families. Migration accelerated to towns due to lack of water and food while competition over the meagre water and grass sources available gave rise to intense tribal conflicts and banditry activities. People are moved to the few places with water and grass.

Response to the urgent situation has stepped up work on several projects to help villagers overcome the crisis. Completion has taken place on several dams and assisted in the maintenance of others. There has been co-ordination for World Food Programmes to assist communities in the construction of feeder roads to improve access to markets and water catchments. Tools, seeds and extension training, including plough use and terracing, has been given to villagers.

Intermediate Technology Development Group

A prayer to accompany the above report:

All-Seeing God

All-Seeing God, through Jesus Christ,
forgive us for the times that we say,
'I can't watch those scenes any longer',
– for the danger of becoming immune to suffering
because it is daily on our television screens–
'I feel powerless;
I have enough to cope with in my own backyard.'

Instead of our resignation
give us the will-power to break out,
through the power of the Holy Spirit,
of our often entrenched ways of living
and give encouragement to the people who are serving.
We know that we can't all up sticks and go,
but, at least, we can support,
through our giving,
the work of the agencies
and the people
who are there in the field.

Prod me now, Lord,
to dig deep into my pocket,
to write a cheque,
to give over my credit card details
to the agency of my choice
which helps our desperate neighbours
in Sudan (*or name another area*)
so that the humanitarian work can be continued.

Thank You, All-Seeing God.
Amen

Geoffrey Duncan

Living Water

Voice One: Creator God, you brought order out of chaos
transforming and separating the raging ocean
into earth, sky and sea
filling them with living creatures;
then you created human beings
and put us in charge of your creation.
Show us how to use your creativity today
when the delicate balance of nature is under
    threat.

Voice Two: Lord Jesus, Living Water
create in each one of us a pool of peace
a deep well of healing that can transform
bitterness to love
impatience to patience
irritation to tolerance
rejection to acceptance
and inadequacy to confidence in our own
    ability.

Voice Three: Holy Spirit, powerful wind moving across the
    waters
enable us to recognize in ourselves
our preoccupation with our own needs and
    desires
our apathy and ignorance in acknowledging
and understanding the needs and desires of
    others.
Empower us to transform this recognition into
    motivation

to seek equality, justice and peace
for all people throughout our world.

Heather Johnston

Drought

Small wind quipples,
Ripples in the cup–
Stippling the cobbles,
Slipping just a sip,
A tantalizing taste . . .
Settling the dust
On the drought-dry crust
Of the summer's heat . . .

Dry leaf skitters,
Scuttles in the gutter–
Unsettled, brittle . . .
Catching at random
In the dirt-dry drain . . .

Old sky mutters,
Echoes from afar . . .
Sun shafts out–
Laughs at the draught,
Puts the rain to rout,
Mocking at the storm–
Perpetuating drought . . .

Desiccating sunshine
Blazing on and on . . .

Old man sighs–
For his harvest is gone . . .

Margot Arthurton

Lord of Life and Love

Lord of Life and Love, thank you for the ways in which we learn from each other in our community. Help us to grow together in our appreciation of each other and to value each one of us for who we are.

Enable us to work together for justice in our community.

Lord of Life and Love, give us fresh insights into the ways in which we use our financial resources. Help us to appreciate the need to re-evaluate our purchasing power and ensure that wherever possible we are supporting people in their local communities.

Enable us to work together for justice in the world.

Lord of Life and Love, give us the spiritual strength to participate in activities which will bring about better living for people in developing nations. Help us in our search for ways to be alongside them looking to Christ as our Leader.

Enable us to be in solidarity with women and men as they help themselves attain a higher standard of living ... as if people and the earth matter.

Lord of Life and Love, lead us to a renewed understanding of what it means for people to be empowered; for our neighbours and our global friends, who live in poverty in their marginalized communities.

Enable us to understand and appreciate the resilient nature of marginalized women and men; to know that all life is valued and to rejoice with them as they continue to become increasingly resourceful people ... as if people and the earth matter.

Lord of Life and Love, open our minds to existing and new ways of caring for people and sustaining Earth. Lead us to discover with people, in partnership, fresh, energetic methods of communicating improved ways for living in remote, barren villages or industrialized, polluted cities.

Enable us to turn around our lifestyles; to become less demanding in our wants and desires so that we are able to experience new ways for living. Awaken our consciences to become pro-active with people wherever they may be . . . as if people and the earth matter.

Geoffrey Duncan

(This prayer may be used in its entirety or each phrase used separately according to the needs of the day.)

Justice and Compassion

God of justice and compassion,

We ask forgiveness for the widening gulf between rich and
    poor,
the use of money as a measure of all things,
the culture of aggressive self-gratification,
the continuing disparities between women and men,
the alienation of disadvantaged communities.

Forgive us for our assumption of a continually improving
    quality of material living,
and our acquiescence in the worship of economic growth,
in a world where resources are limited
and we are already using more than our fair share of some of
    them.

Forgive us for going along with harmful trends because they
   are gradual,
and failing to come to grips with the problems of change and
   complexity.

So fill us with a living faith that we may become lively seeds
   of your kingdom,
growth points in your way of love,
instruments of personal and social reconciliation,
vehicles for a new dawn of spiritual and social liberation.

Lord, in your mercy,
Hear our prayer.

Alan Litherland

... And it Was Very Good

*God saw all that God had made
and it was very good ...*

*Cursed is the ground because of you,
God said to Adam.
In the sweat of your brow you shall eat bread.*

God who made the earth
and saw that it was good,
and trusted it to our care,
we give you thanks for the people who
generations long have tilled the ground
planted and harvested the crops
season by season in want and plenty
tended the livestock early and late
in heat and cold, beauty and bleakness
– and it was very good.

God who made the earth
and said that the ground is cursed
through human sin,
we confess our selfishness and greed
which curse the earth with chemicals
so that we can have cheaper food, higher profits;
which view living creatures as no more
than a means of production to be exploited;
and divide the earth's harvest unequally.
We confess that we enjoy good food at a price
which does not pay a living wage to its producers;
that we are content to close our eyes
to poor working practices, faulty equipment
and toxic chemicals
which endanger life for farm-workers.
Forgive us, and show us how to bless the earth
with loving stewardship.

God whose love redeems all creation,
we pray for farming people whose world is falling apart
because their produce no longer makes a profit
whose livestock is almost worthless because of BSE.
We hold before you those who are at the point of despair,
isolated, seeing no future and no hope.
We pray for rural chaplains and ministers.
We pray for the makers of agricultural policy
in local and regional assemblies,
nationally and internationally,
that care for creation and for human life may be their first
     concern.

God of all creation,
You have given the land and its creatures into our keeping—
teach us to cherish them and use them with kindness
knowing that you mark the falling of a sparrow.
In sharing bread and wine at mealtimes and in sacrament
we remember

that you are Maker of all
and redeem your creation by life-giving love
which is ours through Jesus Christ our Lord.
Amen.

Heather Pencavel

If the Land Could Speak

If the land could speak,
It would speak for us
It would say, like us, that the years
Have forged the bond of life that ties us together.
It was our labour that made her the land she is
It was her yielding that gave us life
We and the land are one!

Kalinga
The Philippines

Quench Our Thirst

O God, pour out on us the water of life that we may quench
our thirst and draw our strength from you. Help us to stand
alongside those who struggle daily for clean water so that all
may be refreshed and renewed by your love.

Water for Life
Christian Aid

Fisher Folk in Kerala

The fisher folk on the coast of Kerala in south India had been
using traditional methods of fishing for centuries. They did
not catch a lot of fish but they caught enough for their own
needs with some left over to sell to villagers further from the
coast.

The fish were kept cool on ice and carried in baskets to the customers.

Then some people from Norway decided to 'help' the fisher folk. They wanted to improve the food supply by increasing the fish catch. They brought modern steel and fibreglass fishing boats, electronic fish finding devices, deep freeze facilities and vans to carry the fish to markets.

The local people no longer caught their own fish. A few were employed on the fishing but the system was so different that it really needed people with skills in industrial fishing. For the most part the villagers had to buy fish rather than eat what they caught themselves.

All the new technology cost money which meant that the price of fish went up. It became too expensive for the local people to buy.

Christian Aid and CAFOD

The Forest is Our Livelihood

The forest is our livelihood. We have lived here before any of you outsiders came. We fished in clean rivers and hunted in the jungle. We made our sago meat and ate fruit trees. Our life was not easy but we lived it in content. Now the logging companies turn rivers into muddy streams and the jungle into devastation. The fish cannot survive in dirty rivers and wild animals will not live in devastated forests. You took advantage of our trusting nature and cheated us into unfair deals. By your doing, you have taken away our livelihood and threaten our very lives. We want our ancestral land, the land we live on, back. We can use it in a wiser way. When you come to us, come as guests with respect.

The Penan People
Borneo

Give, Act and Pray

From my wealth and poverty,
I want to live your jubilee.

Help me to give, act and pray
to share your good news:

for the poor–
release from unpayable debt;

for the rich–
freedom from the power of money.

Rebecca Dudley
Christian Aid

Reflections on the Land

At the heart of everything is the land. The land is my mother.
Like a human being, the land gives us protection, enjoyment
and provides for our needs. We belong to the land in the sense
that it is part of us. Just as you need your home and place, and
protect it, we need our land and want to look after it.

Australian Aboriginal
Christian Aid and CAFOD

What do the forests bear? Soil, water and pure air. Soil, water
and pure air, sustain the earth and all she bears.

Women of Chipko Movement, India
Christian Aid and CAFOD

Climate Change

Here we stand, Creator God.
Forgive us when we treat this beloved planet
as if we own it and can use it as we wish.
Forgive us when we recklessly exploit its resources and
    pollute its complex ecosystems.
Our lifestyle of wasteful over-consumption
in the rich industrial countries is insensitive
to the effects of global warming on
peoples and ecosystems around the world.
We want to express our love and care for all creation.
We know that we must learn more about the problem and
    take effective action.
Here we stand wondering and confused
because of the bounty that you have given us.
And here we stand, Creator God,
and we ask you to help us to care for the earth
as our responsibility.
Help us to do what we know we must
even at the cost of reducing our lifestyle
so that others may live.
Please help us, O God.

The Uniting Church in Australia

Divine Artist and Painbearer

O Divine Artist and Painbearer, open our hearts both to the
destruction which we have inflicted upon nature and also to
the pain which we have heaped upon your heart as its creator.
Help us to weep with the fallen trees, mourn for exterminated
species, be revolted by the rape of Earth itself and in so doing
commit ourselves to the cause of promoting sustainable use of
the world's resources and the preservation of habitat for all
earth's plants and creatures.

William L. Wallace
Aotearoa New Zealand

Reflections

The prosperity of the rich must be replaced by the prospering of all life.

For the rich poverty is obscene,
for the poor wealth is obscene,
for God both are obscene.

Material poverty tends to unite.
Material wealth tends to separate.

There is no peace without justice
and no justice without sharing.

Getting it right for the rich is normally getting it wrong
for the poor.

The economic trickle-down effect from rich to poor does not occur significantly until the dams of power and privilege are breached.

The blood of the prophets is the hope of the poor.

If you want to see the ugly face of the first world,
make a pilgrimage to the third world and see what we have done through colonialism, economic and ecological exploitation.

William L. Wallace
Aotearoa New Zealand

Regeneration

Like fires
that cremated
irreplaceable
flora and fauna,

77

rage and guilt
burnt my heart
but cannot
rewrite history
until earth becomes
our placenta
and this raped soil
our tabernacle:
for liberation grows from the land,
nurturing from the womb of nature
and without beauty or feeling
justice and wisdom
are consumed
by those incinerating gods
Profit, Power and Paternalism.

William L. Wallace
Aotearoa New Zealand

Dearth

And if the planet suddenly sucked and sipped
like a desperate infant, swollen in the heat,
swallowed streams and fountains, wells and falls,
and caused a fateful dryness all around . . .

and if we watched the river beds emerge,
saw dust blow sharply on abrading wind,
saw fish writhe, and the secret life of cool
waters suffer, gasp and die . . .

and if we stood on bridges over nothing,
staring down at acreage of drought,
turned taps and felt that nothing on our fingers,
stuck our heads in rain butts echoing empty . . .

would we congregate in cities to mourn souls
blowing to nowhere, would we pray for rain,
would we save our last drops like treasure
to share, dig down to reservoirs in faith

of liquid being there? Or would we change
the channel on TV, away from sad faces,
as usual, and watch the image of inane
laughter roll around our stagnant brains?

Anne Richards

What's It Worth?

To read: 1 Kings 21:1–21; Luke 7 : 36—8 : 3

Who owns the land?
Some things are not for sale –
my inheritance,
my history,
my identity,
myself.

God of justice, we pray
for people driven off their land
communities destroyed
so that trees can be felled,
the land drilled for minerals,
to put money in the pockets of those who have plenty
at the expense of those who have only themselves
precious and unique.

Who loves the most?
Some things cannot be bought –
my respect
my devotion
my worship
myself.

God of love, we pray
for women abused and exploited
excluded and despised
by those who have used them
and by respectable society,
which turns a blind eye to exploitation
and refuses to speak on behalf of the powerless
who have only love to give.

Teach us to build a community and a world
where everyone is valued justly
and loved freely.

Heather Pencavel

The Sinned Against

Rain, here, there, the skeletal
cattle graze as they can.
Gullies' cheeks crack. Gutted
small-holders harvest dearth.

Rain, here; there, the sinned-against
sun-beat dust infiltrates
brain-cells and sandals, fails
the harvest, yellows the earth.

Over the land there is cloud,
thunder, even, but no rain.
The allotment of pain
is independent of worth.

Drummers, dancers, take drought
and flash-spate in their stride,
laugh at the worst, and smoke
demons out with their mirth;

scratch the ground still for mealies
as goats, dogs, flake at their feet.
The dead speak through the living
in whom hope has its rebirth.

Brian Louis Pearce

From Dry Mass I

In the desert, there's no
water. For the fleshed soul there
is no water. On the
tongue there is none. Water-less
wits wander, go
down the brain-gutter where
the freshest thought stinks, the
screw turns without quarter.

In the glare of the mirage
the sleepy traveller will toss,
denied the oasis;
dream of the wells, the palms,
he thinks will fulfil, the large
tanks and amphorae, the gloss
of wine, the small chalice,
cool arms, breezes like psalms,

the rushes, the papyri
pithy in pools, the loll
in pools icy or steamy.
Tossed night. No use. Can't sleep.
The under sheet mummies me.
Get up. Give up. The whole
creation travails till the
dawn visions hills, sleet on sheep.

Brian Louis Pearce

From Dry Mass II

Rain washes the stains on
old pillars. Christens an old
rogue. Raises the Sphinx out
of sand, women from salt,
snow kings from char. The one-time
Eden's restored. The bowled
love-olive revives. The sprouting
fig-sprig thrives to a fault.

The air is moist-massed again.
The reapers of hope long
deferred leap with the showers,
clap, cup their hands. Clouds tower,
surprise us with prayed rain,
sculpt loveliness, pour song
in clay ears. Grief-burnt hours
green in an instant, flower.

Brian Louis Pearce

Wendover

Are there hands that would destroy
Slow-maturing loveliness?
Mary's foliage and tower;
Heron Water's peacefulness?

Hills above the harvest town
Sheltering its gentleness;
Ancient, wooded Coombe. Will we
Burn the trees of fruitfulness?

Let our barren fingers come
To St Mary's peacefulness:
Shape our fallow years to some
Slow-maturing loveliness.

Brian Louis Pearce

Prayers from the Countryside

From the stench of organo-phosphates
       on summer evenings
From pesticides on our food

O God, deliver us.

From spinners spreading pesticides
       on flowerless green deserts
            where no bird sings
From spraypacks delivering death to meadow thistles
     and butterflies
From the grubbing out of dry stone walls
       and ancient hedgerow habitats

O God, deliver us.

From nuclear fall-out and contamination
From miscarriage, low sperm counts,
            deformity and illness
From diseased fish and poisoned shellfish
From polluted water and frogless ponds

O God, deliver us.

For pigs reeking in intensive squalor
For battery hens confined in featherless servitude
For milk cows bred into obscene deformity
For breeding birds and mammals destroyed by silage
   machinery
For flowerless,
      treeless,
            overgrazed uplands

O God, forgive us.

O God, may we see in our time pigs in coppiced woodlands,
cows in wildflower meadows,

curlews and skylarks in lowland pastures,
hens in orchards
and teeming fish in clean waters.
May we leave for our children a safe, clean and free
    environment,
a world where health and beauty count for more than
    financial gain.
Amen.

Marlene Phillips

Prayer of Confession

Praise to You, Creator of All Things Living, for the restless
power of the wind, the warm energy of the sun, the steady
flow of a waterfall, and the spirit of living things as they return
to clay. How many and wonderful are your works, O Loving
Creator.

We confess that we have forgotten our interconnection with
    your universe.
We confess that we have been indifferent to the
    environmental crises that
    loom large on the horizon of our survival.
We confess that we, our sisters, brothers and children, have
    abused your creation
    through ignorance, exploitation, and greed.
We confess doing permanent damage to your handiwork.
We confess to alienating ourselves from the Source of All Life.
We confess that we have forgotten who we are.
We confess . . . (*Please add your own*)

Forgiving Creator, awaken us to the roaring of creation, the
cries for ecojustice, that we may open our minds and hearts to
respond.

Diann Neu
USA

Words of Wisdom

Wisdom is speaking with words of longing
for peaceful living under clear skies,
for growing crops and water fit to drink,
for just wages and fair prices in exchange for goods.
Wisdom is speaking in the voice of the poor:
Forgive us; we have failed to hear and to understand.

Wisdom is speaking with words of challenge;
inviting us to penitence in place of self-righteousness,
calling us to move from sympathy to solidarity,
demanding justice rather than charity.
Wisdom is speaking in the voice of the poor:
Forgive us; we have failed to hear and to understand.

Wisdom is speaking with words of comfort;
offering forgiveness for our greed and affluence,
assuring us that our reckless rush to devastation
can be halted and our care of the earth restored.
Wisdom is speaking in the voice of the poor:
Forgive us; we have failed to hear and to understand.

Wisdom is speaking with words of hope;
promising us that we and the earth can be one,
inspiring us with faith in the power of people working
    together,
giving us a new vision of partnership and co-operation.
Wisdom is speaking in the voice of the poor:
Forgive us; we have failed to hear and to understand.

Help us to hear and understand
that we may share the salvation of the God of the poor.

Jan Berry

85

The Parable of the Bad Burger Bar Owner

There was once a man who owned three burger bars in a poor part of the city. He was a self-made man and proud of it. He'd started from scratch and worked long hours, expecting others who worked for him to do the same.

One day he decided that he had worked hard enough and he'd have a long holiday; take his wife to see their family in Australia. Before he went he appointed three managers for the three burger bars. He called them together and said: 'Now look here, I'm leaving these burger bars for you to manage while I'm away. I want you to do a good job, as if I was managing them myself. When I get back I expect those burger bars to be running just like they are now and if not then I'll have something to say about it.' And he left.

While he was away the three managers managed the burger bars. The first was much like the owner except worse. He realized that if he was to show a profit when the owner returned and make a bit for himself he'd have to be even more ruthless. He cut the wages of the staff and employed more staff without contract. He even employed underage workers. Everyone was expected to work even longer hours and to serve customers even more quickly. People who went off sick from the stress were sacked without notice and, as he'd already got rid of the union representative and the Chaplain to Marginal Workers, they had no recourse.

The second manager was much the same and he too found ways around the law so that he could get as much as he could out of the burger bar. He bought in cheap meat and some people wondered if it was fit for human consumption. He used genetically modified ingredients and didn't declare them. But once again the workers had no recourse to justice.

The third manager was shocked by what he found when he took up the job and gradually it dawned on him that only he could do something about the unjust situation in the burger bar. He called the Chaplain for Marginal Workers and asked for help in respect of the minimum wage regulations, maternity pay and the like. He got an environmental health officer down to the burger bar and began to improve facilities. The workers were a bit wary of him and still thought he might betray them to the owner so they didn't really trust him, although absenteeism did go down a bit and people agreed they preferred working there in the new conditions.

Then the owner came back from his holiday. He called the managers together and asked them how the burger business was going.

The first manager said: 'You asked me to manage a burger bar which was making £500 a week profit. Well, I've doubled your profit. It's now making £1,000 a week.'

'Well done,' said the owner. 'You're a good manager – you can work for me again!'

The second manager said: 'You asked me to manage a burger bar which was making £200 a week profit. Look, it's now making £400!'

'Well done,' said the owner. 'You're also a good manager and can work for me again.'

The third manager came and said: 'I know you're a hard man but I was appalled at what I found at the burger bar. Workers' rights being disregarded. Health and safety standards ignored. It was dreadful and needed putting right. I've tried to make some improvements and as a result you're lucky that we're still breaking even.'

The owner was angry with the third manager and called him, 'an interfering twit' and 'who did he think he was making all these decisions without authority from him' and 'a bit of hard work never hurt anyone', and so on.

And then he dismissed him there and then saying: 'Ha, ha, now you're unemployed with no reference from me what kind of job do you think you'll get?'

Now the third manager had a home and family to support and he realized things would be grim. He wondered what kind of reception he'd get at the Job Centre and if any of the burger bar workers would speak up for him if he took his case to an industrial tribunal for unfair dismissal.

The workers at the third burger bar were puzzled about what had happened to the manager. They began to talk amongst themselves, quietly of course so as not to raise suspicion. They had never liked the owner but they were afraid to cross him. Should they support the third manager at the industrial tribunal or not?

One of the workers who got maternity benefit because of what the manager had done said: 'We owe that manager a lot. He made our jobs bearable and helped us at considerable risk to himself.' And some of the others agreed although some were wary.

If you have a mouth then use it!

Janet Lees

Harvest Prayer of Confession

God of compassion and infinite mercy,
we need your compassion,
and we are in desperate need of your mercy:
because our compassion fails
and our mercy is severely rationed.

Our fellow human beings
– our neighbours–
are treated unjustly
while we live on the products of their labour.

Our fellow human beings die of hunger
while we have, and eat, more than enough.

Forgive us our helplessness,
as well as our carelessness.

Forgive us the hurt we do not feel
for those who suffer cruelty and oppression;
and the sorrow we fail to share

88

with those whose lives are cut short,
through human violence
or natural disaster.

By your compassion, increase ours;
by your mercy, make us merciful;
make us feel the compassion of Christ,
who dies for it;
and give us power to proclaim,
in word and deed,
the mercy of Christ,
who prays for those who crucify him.

Alan Gaunt

Harvest Time

It's harvest time but there's hunger in the land.
God is working now to help us understand
that the roots of pride go deep in our nation's heart;
let the hardness melt in tears – make a different start.

Repeat

When we've set ourselves above the nations,

Forgive us, Lord.
Forgive us, Lord.

For our dominating and excluding,

Forgive us, Lord.
Forgive us, Lord.

To a joyful sense of who we are,

Revive us, Lord.
Revive us, Lord.

To a Christlike generosity,

Revive us, Lord.
Revive us, Lord.

89

For wars that maim the generations

> Forgive us, Lord.
> **Forgive us, Lord.**

To the reigning of the flag of peace,

> Revive us, Lord.
> **Revive us, Lord.**

To a language through which God can speak,

> Revive us, Lord.
> **Revive us, Lord.**

It's harvest time – rain your Spirit on the land!
Thank you, Lord, for grace to hear and understand.
Let the roots of truth go deep in our nation's heart,
and repentance nourish hope – make a different start.

Repeat

Jenny Dann

Love Your Neighbour

Luke 10 : 25–37

Chorus: Love your neighbour, Love your neighbour,
As you love yourself:
Help each other, help each other,
That's what Jesus said.

Repeat

Here's a story 'bout a traveller
Not so long ago:
Robbers caught him – beat him – left him
Lying in the road.
People came by – priest and Levite–
But they wouldn't stay;
It's easier to close our eyes
And simply walk away.

90

Chorus

Came a stranger on a donkey
From a foreign land;
When he saw a helpless traveller
He stopped to lend a hand:
Cared for him and gave him shelter
Till he was well again–
Because he had an open heart
To feel another's pain.

Chorus

Jesus said, now who was neighbour
To that wounded man?
Yes, it was the one who cared,
The Good Samaritan.
You, like him, must break the barriers
Of hatred, fear and pride;
And when somebody needs you
Don't walk on the other side.

Chorus

Jenny Dann

My Right Can Be Your Wrong

Claiming my rights
can do so much wrong to you:
I demand endless supplies of your fuel,
whose emissions destroy your environment.
I want cheap coffee and tea,
produced at your expense.
I covet alligator gear,
then weep crocodile tears
at animals hunted to extinction.

What I think I need
too often forms my picture
of what is my right,
of what is my due.
And there is very little room left
in that scenario for you.

Righteous God,
take away the selfishness and fear,
that makes me reach out
with grasping hands
to take what is more than my rightful share.
Give me, instead,
a vision that is turned outward
to the needs of theirs;
and a mind and heart
that wants their rights
more than I desire my own.

Susan Hardwick

Vineyard Song

Isaiah 5:1–7; Matthew 21:33.

This is the song of the vineyard; this is the song of the vine.
God dug the soil for the vineyard and the plants that he
    planted were fine.
He built a tower to guard them, dug a pit to tread grapes for
    the wine;
But for all his care and attention only sour grapes grew on
    that vine.

Vineyard, vineyard, what's gone wrong?
What did I fail to do for you?
Vineyard, vineyard, loved so long,
How can I bear to lose you? (*Repeat*)
But this is what it's coming to.

This is the song of the people; God chose and called them her
   own.
She gave good gifts to the people and let truth and justice be
   known.
She looked to them for reflections of the love and the care that
   she's shown;
But she found only cruelty and violence – such a people God
   could not own.

> People, people what's gone wrong?
> What did I fail to do for you?
> People, people loved so long,
> How can I bear to lose you? *(Repeat)*
> But this is what it's coming to.

God sang a song to the vineyard; God sang a song to the vine.
'I'll send my Son to the vineyard and he will reclaim what is
   mine.
Though they reject him and kill him, and refuse every
   teaching and sign,
Yet his death will be life for all people and his Spirit become
   their new wine.'

> Vineyard, vineyard, what's gone wrong?
> What did I fail to do for you?
> Vineyard, vineyard, loved so long
> How can I bear to lose you?
> People, people what's gone wrong?
> What did I fail to do for you?
> People, people loved so long,
> How can I bear to lose you?
> The cross is what it's coming to.

Jenny Dann

Simplistic?

We go in our cars,
We do—
Well, we have to,
We'll be late
Otherwise . . .

It's only a little way,
Lots of stops and starts,
Lots of fumes.

It's hot,
The sun burns
Through the haze—
We can't see far,
Only a little way—
Lots of fumes.

We can't see the sky-hole
The sun burns through—
Because of the haze . . .
We do know it's stopped the rain
Somehow, though—
Not here, but in other places—

Stopped the rain so nothing grows
Over there now . . .
Because we drive our cars here
And the rains stop there—
The crops fail—
So
When we drive here

We steal from their begging bowls.

Margot Arthurton

Best of the Bunch?

Richard Leon, a Costa Rican banana worker, stares out at the plantation which has ruined his health. He is suffering from acute dermatitis across his chest and shoulders and sterility because of his prolonged exposure to pesticides. He is no longer able to work on the plantation and his wife, Teresa, is struggling to make a living by selling food at football matches.

At a neighbouring plantation, Rogelio Lunes rubs the pale blemishes left by pesticides on his cheeks as he describes the intimidation and bullying he has suffered at the hands of his bosses. He is sitting outside the house of his colleague, Arnaldo Fuentes, who is off work because his toes have been rotted by the pesticides which trickle into his boots.

These men are from Batan, in the heart of Costa Rica's banana zone.

'The way they are growing the fruit is totally toxic. It must change. If it is bad for us here, then it must be bad for those who are eating the fruit,' explains another worker who has been left sterile by the pesticides.

Banana farmers pour or spray more than eighteen times the average amount of pesticides used in industrialized countries. Adequate protective clothing is rarely provided and the mist from aerial spraying blows over the nearby houses and gardens. Pesticides have seeped in houses situated on a plantation owned by Chiquita, the United States multinational company. The water has a brown residue. Children suffer from diarrhoea and vomiting.

Christian Aid supports the Syndicate of Workers on Agricultural Plantations (SITRAP) and its sister unions through the Co-ordination of Banana Workers' Unions which is working to improve conditions in banana plantations all over Latin America.

Eighteen-year-old Juana Montenegro managed to hold on to her job throughout her pregnancy but found that Chiquita bosses were very unsympathetic. 'I wanted to change jobs because I was working in the fields and this is very heavy work but during my pregnancy they sent me back into the fields four times. My colleagues were worried about me and said, "Why's she come out into the fields when she's pregnant?" I was worried about my baby but they said that if I didn't go out into the fields there was no work for me.'

Juana returned to work within three months of her son's birth. Because she wasn't allowed to take breaks of more than fifteen minutes, Gabriel, her baby, would go without a breast feed from 6.30 am to 6.30 pm. He was given formula milk, made with the plantation's contaminated water, and became very thin.

Staff at SITRAP are convinced that there must be change: 'It is wrong that just for the sake of banana exports, people are dying, land is left barren or littered with blue plastic and rivers are being poisoned.'

Christian Aid

Sylvester is Four Years Old

Sylvester is four years old. He sits
on the ground outside his hut. He is
too weak to stand any more. In the
distance he sees his father, carrying
a great load of bananas.
The harvest is good.

Sylvester cries out and stretches
his hands towards the beautiful fruit.
but his father walks on and his
mother looks at him sadly.

'We cannot eat the bananas,' she says,
'they are not for us. We have to send
them to the rich people across the sea
because our country owes their country
money.'

Sylvester says nothing. His head droops
and he has no energy to brush away the flies
that cluster around his eyes.

That night, Sylvester dies – of hunger.

Anthea Dove

Banana Workers from Costa Rica

Doris Calvo

Doris first started working in the banana plantations when
she was thirteen years old. Several years later, she decided
to join the union. At that time she was working in the pack-
ing house, as the women often do, and she began talking
to her fellow workers about the benefits that being in the
union can bring. Her bosses overheard her, called her into
the manager's office and sacked her. The company put
her name on a blacklist and when Doris approached other
farms owned by the multinational companies she was refused
work.

Doris refused to leave the union. Later, her family were also
put on the blacklist. Her son was dismissed from a Del Monte
plantation. Doris was forced to learn other trades like mend-
ing shoes in order to survive.

At fourteen she was sexually harassed by her boss as he
was driving her to work. She threw herself out of the car
and escaped covered in mud. In her own words: 'I had a clear
conscience because the earth can be shaken from the body.'

Later Doris commenced work for the Women's Project of
the SITRAP union. She says – apart from the harassment –
the worst problem that the women face is the use of agro-
chemicals.

'The chemicals give them diseases. Their nails drop off, they
get chemical burns on their skin, the chemicals they come into
contact with give them throat and lung problems, foot fungi,

kidney problems and even miscarriages. There's no end to the problems,' said Doris.

Pregnant women also have a particularly difficult time. One woman took time off to see a doctor but when she returned to work she was told that she had been dismissed.

One of the chemicals used some years ago on the plantation, DBCP, was later proved to cause sterility and genetic mutation in pregnancy. One woman on the plantation gave birth to a child so severely deformed that his head was four times bigger than his body and the nose and mouth were joined together.

Banana workers from many countries worldwide took the manufacturers and users of DBCP to court in the United States to claim compensation for being made sterile.

Carlos Mora

Carlos worked for a banana company for over twenty-five years. He then became the union member responsible for ecological affairs.

'Before the plantations this region was exporting rice and maize. Now there is no rice or maize. Most of the plantations aren't going to last beyond 2010. And then we're going to have rivers without fish, poisoned people, contaminated soil, a lot of non-degradable plastic and polluted air. The deserted banana plantations are like deserts. They have to be left fallow for at least thirty years,' says Carlos.

Carlos is one of the 'burnt ones'. He is now sterile because of using the chemical DBCP on the plantations. Also, he suffers from headaches, kidney problems and sometimes loss of sight. People have died as a result of using DBCP.

When the workers were told to use DBCP nobody informed them that it had already been banned in the United States. Carlos was advised to take an out-of-court settlement of US$7,500, enough for only nine days' care in Costa Rica. He is worried that the chemicals in use now on the plantations will turn out to be just as dangerous. He worries most about young people who might use chemicals without protective clothing. Aerial spraying means that these people are sprayed with chemicals while they are at work in the plantations.

'Not only is the poison carried downstream by waterways but it is dragged off to other places by the wind. Whole areas of the population get sprayed by the poison: schools, churches, homes with children and the sick.'

Carlos believes that the only real solution is first to reduce the number of chemicals used on the plantations and then to eliminate their use altogether.

World Development Movement

Giving

If you can give
You can live,
And not count
Nor mount up
Another's debt—
You can forget
And let
Be . . .
For we
All must
Trust—
And to trust
Is to give . . .
And to give
Is to live.

Margot Arthurton

Harvest for the World

6.00 pm in the crypt of St Martin-in-the-Fields, London, on a beautiful, cool autumn evening

An interesting mix of people
   – all ages–
Plenty of lively conversation
An attractive vegetarian menu
Profits go toward the project
   for homeless people.
Hungry people are fed
Distressed people are given shelter
– that's their Harvest,
being fed and given shelter.

God of the (w)holistic Church
God of many satisfied stomachs
We have come in from the real world
to draw breath
to engage in social chit-chat
to wait for family or friends
to have a pleasant evening
at the theatre
but then . . .
where are you, God of Love,
in the wars which tear the world apart?
Where are you, Christ of Compassion,
in the refugee situations
and the ever increasing numbers of devastated people?
Where are you, Holy Spirit of Comfort,
where there is no harvest for millions of people?
In the places where there is hunger
Drought . . . floods . . . poverty
Greed . . . ignorance . . . bigotry.

You are there,
God of Love,
Christ of Compassion,
Holy Spirit of Comfort,
in the normal everyday patterns of life,
and
I know that there are many people in the faith communities;
the humanitarian organizations;
the charities who are working round the clock to alleviate
     suffering
to take a Harvest to suffering people
and then

I give thanks.

People are striving for better days,
for the time when the hungry
and thirsty
shall have their needs met;
for peace and reconciliation,
and where that happens there you are
in the midst,
getting on with life.
Yes – God of Love,
I and many others will stick in there.
Amen.

Geoffrey Duncan

Modelling

Each person is given a small amount of plasticine or modelling
clay and invited to model something from God's creation.
They could, for example, make a tree or an animal. The models
are kept before them as everyone joins in a celebration of the
goodness of creation, in song and prayer.

   After celebrating the goodness of creation, people are

reminded of humanity's destruction and exploitation of nature. To symbolize this they are asked to destroy their models. They then join in an act of confession.

After the act of confession all are given the opportunity to recommit themselves to the care of creation and to promise to take concrete action as an outward sign of this commitment. They are then invited to take their modelling clay and to model a symbol of their proposed action. For example, they could model a tree as a symbol for planting a tree or supporting an organization which protects the rain forest. They could model food as a symbol for supporting fair trading.

Lindsey Sanderson

Puddles and Rainbows

Splattered puddle,
Spectrum swirled,
Spirit spillage,
Ruined world –
Mocking rainbow,
Mocking pearl –
Jettisoned
In feckless haste . . .
Sullied,
Muddied,
Reckless waste . . .
Oiled, soiled
Spoiled soil.

But what of rainbow in the sky?
What of pearl in oyster shell?
Spectrum's light in trembling drop –?

What of these,
Mysterious all –?

Intact, unharmed, perpetual,
Untouched by feckless, reckless waste
They will remain – inviolate . . .
The drop, the pearl, the rainbowed skies–
For there – entire – perfection lies.

Margot Arthurton

Part Four:

Let me be as Christ to you . . .

'Lord, when did we see you hungry and feed you, or thirsty and give you something to drink?'
Matthew 25:37

Right to Health

Too many have died because of starvation,
too many are distressed for lack of pure water.
We should work together, nation and nation,
to ensure that each individual and every family
have enough food to sustain health,
have access to pure water to ensure wholesome living.
There is a right to health and life
since God created the world
with the capacity to meet human needs.
May we work together with God's guidance
that the hungry may be fed
and all the people celebrate abundant life.

Righteous Judge,
your will for your people is fullness of life
and hope for the future.
We confess that we have failed each other
and betrayed our faith
whenever a child lacks essential food,
whenever a family has no access to safe water,
whenever a parent grieves for a starving family.
There is enough food to meet the needs of all
but we waste our scarce resources;
by human conflict we destroy harvests
and lay waste the land.
Forgive us for past failings;
challenge us to present actions
and inspire us for sharing in the future.

Loving Shepherd,
lead us beside still waters,
refresh us in green pastures,
not to enjoy endless retreats
but to equip us to confront injustice,
to stand up for human rights,
to be a voice for the voiceless;
whatever the cost, whatever the pain,
however strong the oppressor,
however threatening the tyrant.
When we declare your word of truth
and unite with your people to oppose tyranny,
there will be plenty for all
and feasting and fun will be a shared celebration.

John Johansen-Berg

When Will the Rains Come?

Lord, I am so comfortable,
the water is running out of our tap
and so near us, just a short bus journey away
there are thousands of families
who don't even have a single drop.

When will the rains come?

Lord, try and open my eyes
to these basic needs of my brothers and sisters.
Keep me from being complacent:
let me not just turn on our tap
and forget their desperate need.

When will the rains come?

Lord, you do not see us as rich and poor,
but as one family,
involved with one another,
bearing each other's burdens,
going the extra mile,
being concerned.

When will the rains come?

I don't know when they will come,
nor do the villagers,
but I do know that I could care more,
and maybe that by caring more
my brothers and sisters
will find new strength
even when the wells are dry.

Peter Millar

Why, God?

The rains have failed.
We see the dry earth:
we see people go hungry, they starve, they die.
Why, God?

The rains are mighty.
We see the plains flood:
we see the people drown, their homes washed away.
Why, God?

Your creation is suffering.
We despair, we are angry, we want to know
why, God?

We know that we are not blameless.

Through our lack of care
we harm nature's balance.
By our unthinking greed, self interest,
your world is spoiled.

We trust you, our God, to show us
how to care for creation.

Alan Baldwin

There is Sickness . . . There is Cholera

The public water supply only comes on for an hour a day in Matagalpa, Nicaragua's third-largest city. Many neighbourhoods have no water at all. Diarrhoea is the biggest killer and cholera – once eradicated – is now commonplace.

Janett Castillo draws water from a bucket to make breakfast and get her family ready for the day ahead. Then she takes her eight-year-old daughter for the morning shift at school, leaves her baby daughter with her mother and heads for work.

Janett runs a small organization in Matagalpa, Nicaragua, called the Community Movement. It helps local community groups to obtain water, sanitation and some health care. The tiny office seems to be open day and night and the demands are never-ending. By the time Janett arrives two of her colleagues are already there, talking to an anxious-looking man from one of the outlying neighbourhoods.

Within an hour, Janett is off to a meeting with the city council about some water pipes it had promised to provide. Typically it is frustrating – more delays, more excuses. She manages to extract a date and commitment before leaving but knows that will not be the end of the story. Off next to visit community leader, Salvador Rajos. On her way Janett goes home to feed her baby then she helps to load up six basic concrete toilets and some bags of cement for the latrine building which is already under way in Salvador's community.

Back at the office someone comes in to buy one of the little locally made ornaments which are sold to help stretch the funds given to them by Christian Aid. Then it is time for the last meeting of the day. Four community health volunteers have come in to plan the next training day. It will include the dangers of stored and dirty water and of puddles of waste water, a breeding ground for mosquitoes which carry malaria and dengue. Volunteers will be encouraged to show people how to cover water supplies and disperse waste water. Simple, effective prevention in action.

This work is not new to Janett. It follow many years unpaid work as a community leader in her own neighbourhood. She is energetic, dedicated and very good at simply getting things done, every day.

'Without water, there is sickness and there is cholera. Without water there is no life.

There were frequent outbreaks of cholera in the neighbour-hood of Las Marias before the water project. Now, cholera has been completely wiped out and far fewer children suffer with diarrhoea. Clean water really makes a difference, fast.

Janett Castillo
Christian Aid

Christ, We Do Not Recognize

Christ, we do not recognize
Your face in all the world;
Neither do we understand
The love to which we're called.

Christ, we do not understand
Compassion's power and course;
Neither do we empathize
With those who need its force.

111

Christ, we do not empathize
When dearth confronts our greed;
Neither do we recognize
Love longs to meet that need.

Andrew Pratt

Change My Ways

I own an orchard
but I won't give you an apple.
I cultivate a beanfield
and sell you soya at a good profit.
I have an education.
I use it to put one over on you.
My shelves are full of books.
I won't teach you to read.
You have drought and I have rain.
It spoils my day.
I glory in bright silks to wear
but give you cast-offs.
I have much to learn
Will you teach me?

Angela Topping

Many of Us Struggle to Lose Weight

Lord, we know we live in a divided world:
while we enjoy the fruits and beauty of the countryside,
others toil with parched and barren soil
or floods;
many of us struggle to lose weight,
while others know nothing but hunger.
Help us to find ways to redress the balance
and to show we care.

Philippa Harbin/Christian Aid

School, Coffee and Squash

Pebronilla Namboko, her husband, son and grandchildren live in Bududa, a village in eastern Uganda. She loves children – she is a mother, a grandmother and a primary school teacher.

She and her husband have a *shamba*, a piece of land on which she grows vegetables, beans, maize and bananas. Also, she grows coffee which is sold to the Uganda Coffee Marketing Board (CMB) in the town of Mbale. The CMB sells the coffee on the world market but when the world price fell they could not pay the Namboko family. Earning this money was the only way Pebronilla could afford to send the children to school. All the schools charge fees because the government does not have enough money for free schooling. As she couldn't depend on coffee she started to grow passion fruit as well. She got a loan to buy seedlings, poles and barbed wire for the passion fruit creepers to grow on. She sells the fruit in the local market and to Hajati Jameela who lives in Mbale and makes wonderful passion fruit squash.

With the money she earns she can help with school fees for the grandchildren but she could not do this without the *shamba*.

Christian Aid

A Peruvian Woman

Antidora Sulca is a Peruvian woman who has suffered much through years of civil war, the loss of her home and family and continuing poverty because of very high prices for basic food. Her harvest is almost non-existent but the spirit of these Peruvian women will not be crushed.

We shall not be crushed;
we do not despair;
we know you will never abandon us;

113

or let us be destroyed:
for you are the God of life,
and we carry your life in us.

Christian Aid

Impartial God

Impartial God, you cause the rain to fall
on the good and the bad,
the just and the unjust,
the righteous and the unrighteous.

We praise you for the rain:
    for the life-giving rain which enables food to grow
    and crops to yield their harvest so that the world may be
        fed;
    for the cleansing rain which refreshes the air we breathe,
    clears the dust from dirt paths, and washes the grime
        from the city streets;
    for the thirst-quenching rain which fills rivers and lakes,
    reservoirs and water tubs,
    so that all may have enough to drink;
    for the cooling rain which relieves the scorching heat of
        the day.

        Be glad, O people of Zion.
        Rejoice in the Lord your God.

Refreshing and life-giving God,
    come as the life-giving rain to bring harvests where there
        is barren land,
    fertility where there is dust and sand;
    come as the cooling rain to dampen the heat of anger and
        hatred
    between race and race, sect and sect, nation and nation;
    come as the rain of justice, to free the oppressed and those
        enslaved

114

by economic systems which exploit the weak for the sake
    of the strong;
come as the peace-giving rain to nations at war
and to armies engaged in an uneasy truce.

Be glad, O people of Zion.
Rejoice in the Lord your God.

May the abundant showers of your grace
fall on all peoples and all nations,
that your world may be one in justice, in plenty, and in peace.

'Active Power'

The Story of the Dogon People: Mali

*Successive droughts and the advance of the Sahara desert have hit
traditional water sources on the Dogon Plateau. After centuries of
survival in this harsh land, the Dogon people were leaving in droves.
This is a story of hardship, tenacity and success.*

The Dogon Plateau in northern Mali is fifty miles wide and
runs for about one hundred and thirty miles north to south.
Arid and hostile, the land is literally made of bedrock with
high cliffs eroded into strange rock formations. There is very
little soil and few trees. Finding water has always been a
struggle. Mali has one of the hottest climates in the world and
temperatures on the Dogon Plateau are among the hottest in
Mali, averaging around 104° F or 40°C.

Survival on the plateau requires an exceptional blend of
stubbornness and tenacity combined with skill and sheer hard
work. The Dogon people are well known for their innovative
techniques of vegetable growing, terracing and irrigation systems. These have enabled them to create fertile vegetable plots
on solid rock.

Until relatively recently the Dogon people were isolated
from outside influence, protecting their rich culture. Then

during the 1970s and 1980s the plateau was hit by a series of severe droughts. Thousands of people finally gave up the struggle to survive on the plateau and left. With diminishing crops those who remained were forced to adapt and to open up to the outside world.

Against all odds and with a little help from outside, the story of the Dogon people continues to this day. In need of a cash crop to supplement the food they grow, the Dogon have specialized in growing onions in the little patches edged with stone. Trees are being planted and the full benefits of slightly better rainfall are being utilized with dams and careful schemes for retaining water and soil. With clean water from wells there are far fewer cases of parasites, diarrhoea and the painful guinea-worm which used to be so prevalent.

The Catholic Mission of Bandiagara has been sinking wells and creating small dam constructions and pumps. Bandiagara is working with fifteen villages to train two members of each water committee in basic maintenance and repair of their manual pumps. As the work progresses it is becoming more holistic with an integrated approach to helping people solve their other problems. The work includes:

- health, emphasizing preventive medicine at a household level;
- women's activities, including small co-operatives and credit systems;
- children's literacy through centres in fifteen villages;
- sustainable agriculture with demonstration plots, training and open days.

Bandiagara is using appropriate technology and plans to encourage village organizations and participation.

Christian Aid

116

Rukmani's Story: the Himalayas, North India

For centuries women in the Himalayan foothills of northern India have collected water for their families from isolated water-holes, known as naulas. These are often a long way from people's homes and are heavily polluted by animals and sewage. In recent years the situation has become much worse as mining, logging and construction have led to soil erosion. With few trees and little grass water flows downhill very quickly and is not stored. Women spend hours every day finding water, firewood and fodder for their animals.

The Kassar Trust has introduced low-cost well-technology suitable for the Himalayan foothills. With their water problem solved, local people are now working with Kassar Trust to protect and improve their environment.

Rukmani is forty years old and lives in the scattered community of Sorag village near the Tibetan border. She and her husband and two of their four children share a traditional stone house with two other families. They rely for survival on money sent back by their two sons who left the area in search of paid work. This supplements the food they can grow on their small plot of land.

In common with most women, Rukmani is up at around 5.00 am every morning to light the fire and cook roti and vegetables for breakfast. Unlike other women, however, she overcame her natural shyness and was the first to join the Sorag *samity* (village committee) set up to work with Kassar Trust. Women have always been responsible for finding water and Rukmani saw the need for women to be involved in the plans to bring water to their village.

'Our first task was to tackle health problems in the village. Sewage was polluting sources of drinking water and making people ill. With help from Kassar Trust, we built protected wells and toilets.'

From there the community moved on and Rukmani has seen many changes in the past five years. She is particularly enthusiastic about the women's increasing knowledge and self-confidence. They started a *balwadi* (playgroup) scheme for the children. To begin with parents were suspicious but now they send their children. This has brought the parents closer together and they are now pressing for solar lighting so that their children can read at night. Rukmani spends many hours walking along steep, winding tracks in her role as co-ordinator of the *balwadi* in seventeen local villages.

She has made such an impact that she is being encouraged to stand for election as a representative of the community. Whilst it would be a great loss if she left the *samity* the election of a local woman would bring great prestige and pride to the village and an all-important voice.

Christian Aid

Put Love in the Heart

We beseech you, Lord, to put love and kindness
in the hearts of people everywhere
especially those who seek to
exploit the needs of others
for their own gain and also
the war-lords and chiefs
who create situations of hunger, famine and poverty,
making people vulnerable and easy to exploit.
We ask you also, Lord, to put understanding in the hearts
of those lawmakers in the wealthier countries
who create situations not to the common good,
putting a false bottom in the market,
forcing a pattern at home and in the world
where a few have everything and
the majority almost nothing.
Through him who lived amongst the
'have nots', Jesus Christ.
Amen

Source Unknown
An African Prayer/Fair Trade

God of Justice

God of justice, manifest in a carpenter's son,
we pray for all who labour and toil
and for those charged with
protecting the conditions of their work.
Grant to these stewards of economic justice
an abiding and untiring
commitment to the rights of all workers
and to the protection of international
labour standards throughout the world.
Amen.

Source Unknown

From the Cradle to the Grave

Purchase Fairly Traded tea and coffee from the harvest in Tanzania – it could help people like Esther and her family. Harvest is inextricably tied up with health. Enjoy your coffee and tea.

Esther has two children, David and Joyce. During the labour with her first child, David, the health clinic in Mavala was not built so she tried to reach the hospital in the next village which is nine kilometres away.

'I started to walk to the hospital but failed and came back.'

Often there is no access to medical care during and after the birth of their babies so Tanzanian women face a risk of death which is fifty times greater than women in northern Europe. However, concerns for her new daughter take precedence over concerns for herself:

'I don't know whether my child will grow up and reach adulthood. She may get ill and die. There is nothing I can do about it. Some children are going to die young.'

The family managed to raise the £4.00 fee for Joyce's delivery at the hospital. Even so, baby Joyce is fourteen times more likely to die in her first year than babies born in Britain.

People will really struggle to get the money if their child gets ill. You just can't leave your child if it is sick, can you?

Christian Aid

Malnourished

Over 200 million children in developing countries under the age of five are malnourished. For them, and for the world at large, this message is especially urgent. Malnutrition contributes to more than half of the nearly 12 million deaths in developing countries each year. Malnourished children often suffer the loss of precious mental capacities. They fall ill more often. If they survive, they may grow up with lasting mental or physical disabilities. This human suffering and waste happen because of illness – much of it preventable; because breast-feeding is stopped too early; because children's nutritional needs are not sufficiently understood; because long-entrenched prejudices imprison women and children in poverty. The world knows what is needed to end malnutrition. With a strong foundation of co-operation between local communities, non-governmental organizations, governments and international agencies, the future – and the lives of our children – can take the shape we want and they deserve, of healthy growth and development, greater productivity, social equality and peace.

Kofi Annan
United Nations

Shared Interest

Shared Interest is a co-operative lending society which gives people in the UK the opportunity to invest positively in Third World enterprises that will benefit poorer people and their communities. Opening an account with Shared Interest is about being a part of a movement for change; a change to the present unjust system of world trade and finance and a change in the lives of those who are not being given a fair chance. Whether you invest the maximum £20,000 or the minimum £100 you take a stand against injustice and help to change the world.

The Cheque's in the Post

The aim of Shared Interest's Micro-credit Bond was to raise £1.3 million within four months for micro-credit; £400,000 of that for new lending and £900,000 to refinance our existing loan of £2 million to the Ecumenical Development Co-operative Society for their micro-credit lending in the Third World. In the event we raised nearly twice as much new money as we had intended and had regretfully to send back £368,900. We apologize to those of you who could not understand why your cheques had to be sent back.

Shared Interest

Agnes

Agnes looks to be in her late 50s but it is difficult to tell. She could be much younger; sixteen years of bloody civil war in which her eldest daughter was killed and the long painful process of trying to rebuild her life since the peace accord was signed in 1992 have etched deep lines of pain and weariness on her face. Agnes lives in a part of eastern Mozambique which saw some of the fiercest fighting. During the war, tens of thousands of people fled. Roads, bridges, shops, schools and hospitals were destroyed either by explosives or by a decade of sheer neglect. With little remaining intact and their houses destroyed, Agnes and her neighbours have to start from scratch. As a widow bringing up three children alone, Agnes represents one of the very poorest sectors of this economically marginalized region. Agnes dreams of her own bicycle but the only ones in the village belong to men. Her

son-in-law has a bicycle and offers to take some of her produce
to sell in Malawi which is over three days' cycle ride away.

Christian Aid

A Question of Judgement

'Let there be light!'
you said
And so you set apart
day from night–
just as,
on Judgement Day,
you have told us how
you will sift the wheat from the chaff
in your, heavenly harvest.

But are not the no-good, throw-away parts
just as important to you?
Does it not go
against the grain
of your compassion and mercy,
to keep the best
but to bin the rest?

To act in this way,
is what we humans would do–
but surely not *you*.
How can you destroy
that which you have created?
The chaff may be useless,
but surely it has the same yearning for life
As the nourishing wheat.

Does not the darkness
make great the anticipation of the dawn?
And does not the chill
of the most bitter night,
emphasize the warmth of the following day?
When you created the light,
you also created night
and even named it so;
thus giving it an identity
and a special place
in your Creation.

Perhaps it is my own case I plead.
For when I die I shall see
how really it is
that you have perceived me.
How will you judge my harvest, I wonder:
as useless chaff—
or as life-giving grain?

Help me,
Creator God,
through all my confusion and seeking,
to a harvest of wisdom
and of understanding.
For I have to confess that,
hitherto,
my own experience of you
does not accord
with a God who puts
anger over forgiveness,
judgement over compassionate love.

Susan Hardwick

Creator and Provider

God, the Creator and Provider, we confess the miserable failure of our human mechanisms for sharing the resources and opportunities of the earth. Give us, we pray, the insight to see the global rich/poor divide for what it really is, the skill to persuade opinion-formers and decision-makers of that truth and the integrity to accept for ourselves whatever limitations our gospel of sharing implies.

Grant to our own and other governments a vision of a just and caring world, the courage to move towards that vision with decisive action, and the ingenuity to work out new ways for bridging the gulf of poverty and debt.

Help us, through the Fair Trade movement, to find ways of using consumer power to by-pass bureaucracy so as to bring justice to primary producers in the developing world.

Alan Litherland

Beyond Fishing

Christian Community Services (CCS) was formed by the Anglican Church of Kenya in the dioceses of Kitale and Eldoret in 1985 as the development department of the church. CCS has various programmes all of which were built on the Chinese proverb: 'Give a man a fish and you feed him for a day. Teach a man to fish and you feed him and his family for a long while.' Now, however, the programmes face a new challenge – the upstream of the river is getting polluted by more powerful people, and fish downstream are dying, leaving the poor without fish.

World Council of Churches

God's Generosity

God, you heap your love upon us
        like a mother providing for her family's need,
        embracing her child with tenderness.
Forgive us
        when, like spoilt children,
        we treat your generosity as our right,
        or hug it possessively to ourselves.
Give us enough trust to live securely in your love
        and to share it freely with others
        in open-handed confidence
        that your grace will never run out.

Jan Berry

Harvest Festival

Mrs Forster baked a wondrous loaf
with many decorations, for the feast.
Mr Barker brought a case of wine
back from France – 'It's rather good,' he said –

and the tickets cost only a pound.
They broke the bread together and they drank
and talked about the restoration fund.
The vicar said they'd all done very well.

Jesus, sitting in the hall, invisible,
dropped his crust to the dog tied up
by the door, shared his fruit
with the crying kid in the pram,

and watched the local tramp slink by
mumbling, with his cart of cast-off things,
and wondered that a tear escaped his eye
at the state of the restoration fund.

Anne Richards

125

Feed the Poor

'Feed the poor,
Aid the victims
But don't ask questions,'
The rulers said.
'Don't ask how they became poor,
Who benefits from their poverty
Or how the rich/poor gap widens.'
'Remember,' the rulers said,
'The economists are right.'
I said,
'Right out!
Right out of their hearts!
Right out of their gut!
Right out of their minds!
For their minds have become
Disembodied,
Disembowelled,
And there is no connectedness,
No wholeness.'
Outside and inside of the Church
The Babel Tower of the Market-Place
Is worshipped in the new temple
With the God-like face—
The temple of simplistic ideology
And economic fundamentalism—
The temple which offers the illusion
That the poor are the problem
Not the rich.
'My God, my God
Why have you forsaken me?'
Cry the poor.
And God replies,
'I have not forsaken you;

With you I hang on the cross
Made by politicians, economists
And multinational executives.
For at this moment the devil has two right wings.'

William L. Wallace
Aotearoa New Zealand

Compassionate Lord

We remember before you
People whose lives are destroyed by disaster
Families whose homes have been devastated
Villages in remote, rural situations in developing countries
        where there is drought, poverty, and marginalization
Indigenous people who flee destruction
        due to man-made disasters caused by greed.

Pause for reflection

Lord, help us to accept some of the responsibility for the
oppression in people's lives when we shop irresponsibly in
the local supermarket. When we purchase food which sup-
posedly tastes more supreme or which smells more delicious
or for the colour on our plates, having total disregard for the
slavery instigated to support our shallow lifestyles.

We pray for people employed in the banana trade, especially the exploited, underpaid farmers and the women, men
and children exposed to life-harming pesticides, remembering
that multinational corporations control the majority of trade
and promote the evil side of globalization.

Help us to search our hearts
Help us to search our minds

So that we discover the benefits for our partners, through Fair
Trade and Fairly Traded items.

Compassionate Christ,
> **where families are bound by fear**
> **where families starve**
> **where families die for lack of clean**
> > **drinking water**
>
> **Enable us to stand up and be counted;**
> > **to be the people of your Radical Church**
> > **and to break the chains of oppression.**

Geoffrey Duncan

Volunteering

They say collecting
(Door to door)
Is a thankless task;
Not so!
Time-consuming, yes,
But never thankless.
So many people
Love to give
Their notes and coins
To help others
Live a healthier life;
Making wells, and
Planting crops in fields
Offering hope and freedom.

Some who give are more prepared
Than others,
Envelopes filled and sealed.
Some dilly-dally—
Momentary forgetfulness concealed:
'Where did I put that envelope?
It should be here behind the clock:

Who's moved it?
Oh, there it is beside the phone.
Sorry to keep you, hope you do well!'

Wendy Whitehead

Collecting for Charity

Oh no! It's that time of year again.

I hope I don't call on too many houses with noisy dogs. Lord help me to answer questions like 'I'm not a Christian, so why should I help?'

No-one asked me why they should help but many people from other faiths gave me their envelopes.

Lord, help me not to feel angry at those who say 'no'; at those who are too busy watching their expensive televisions to answer; at those who drive off in their posh cars when I arrive; at those who say that they can't give because there is nobody in.

Lord, help me to respond to those who want a political answer – and to those who think that Christians should not be involved in politics.

Lord, thank you for those who give as much as they can and for the jokers who cheer me up by offering a phone book, a carrier bag and the kitchen stool as well as filling up their envelope.

Lord, thank you for those who feel sorry for a wet, bedraggled and windblown collector, but could we have some sunshine next year please?

Lord, thank you for my friends who collect with me and for those who support me with prayer.

Lord, I'm glad I was able to help.

Alan Baldwin

Shivagami

Shivagami and her husband, Manoharan, work as tea pickers on an estate in north India. She works very hard, constantly leaning forward to pluck the fragile leaves. Since the estate was bought by a company which sells its tea to Clipper Teas their life has improved.

Before the estate was bought Shivagami earned 15 rupees a day. This was not enough to buy basic food. She worked long hours every day. There was no time to look after the one room where the family live. There was no school for the children. She could have lost her job at any time.

Since the estate was bought by the new company Shivagami works from 8.00 am until 4.00 pm and has time to do other jobs at home. She earns 50 rupees a day. There is enough money for basic food. There is a 'fair price shop' where she can buy things cheaply. Her family live in their own cottage. There is a primary school on the tea estate. She has a contract for her work.

Christian Aid

The Great Feast of Life

O God, you promise a world
where those who now weep shall laugh;
 those who are hungry shall feast;
 those who are poor now,
 and excluded,
 shall have your kingdom for their own.
I want this world too.
I renounce despair.
I will act for change.
I choose to be included
in your great feast of life.
Amen.

Christian Aid

Living with the New Economic Order

God, who calls us to community:
We pray as people committed to a new community in Christ.

For the sake of the poor, your people of old
did not reap to the edge of their field,
or pick up the loose ears,
or the fallen grapes.

But now forests are privatized
and the poor can't pick up fallen branches,
or hunt,
or gather.

The new idol, Profit,
has made thieves of us all.

We proclaim your love and justice.
But we need your help lest we become deceivers,
full of words,
unable to do anything
to strengthen the weak
and share the burden
of those for whom you have a special care.

Have mercy on us.

The Uniting Church in Australia

God of Liberation

God of liberation, whose will it is that the poor should be
raised up,
the captives freed and the impoverished nourished,
help us to work with you for the nurturing of all the life of
earth.

William L. Wallace
Aotearoa New Zealand

131

Help Us to Grow Together, O God

We pray for the indigenous people around the world, especially remembering those in Taiwan, the Philippines, India, Aotearoa New Zealand and elsewhere in Asia and the Pacific. Grant that majority cultures will respect indigenous cultures and allow indigenous people to 'breathe freely', to live in security, with self respect, pride in identity and appreciation of cultural riches.

All: Help us to grow together, O God.

We thank you for the love and care for the earth that indigenous people show, for their attentiveness to the seasons, sun, moon and stars, trees, ants, animals. Help us to learn from this wisdom and live in harmony with your world.

All: Help us to grow together, O God.

Weave us closer O God, that indigenous and non-indigenous may relate without brushing over the hurts and mistakes of the past, but honestly facing them and helping to heal them in a spirit of repentance and openness, that with your help we might create something new together.

**All: Help us to grow together, O God, in love, in respect
       and in friendship. Amen**

The Uniting Church in Australia

Making the Connection

Think of the difference fair trade brings.
The dignity of wages for work that is valued.
Pride in the history of learning to grow,
to carve, to stitch. That sense of purpose.

132

Think of the power of a coffee bean,
the taste of satisfaction. Crops grown,
enjoyed by others, appreciated,
giving the pleasure of making plans.

Think of the fingers that made the stitch,
weaving us together, thread to thread,
touch upon touch, smile meeting smile.
Imagine the dream and feel it taking shape.

Think of connecting hope with reality,
one world with another, lives and hearts
and voices in a joyful celebration.
Rejoice in the difference fair trade brings.

Fiona Ritchie-Walker

Buyers and Sellers

God, you know in our country these people are special;
but no-one can fool you,
neither the buyer nor those that sell.
It is not just a trifle over which we can make merry.
There can be fraud while people are hungry.
Others pile up their riches.
God, whether we buy or sell,
let us stick to this:
we are quite willing to pay the value of the goods
but others should not over-charge.
God, make peace here as well.

Source Unknown
Uganda/Fair Trade

A Coffee Grower's Comment

Without Cafédirect and Fair Trade many coffee growers here could not have continued – the price paid by the middlemen was not enough to cover the cost of growing and preparing it.

Miguel Barrantes
Costa Rica

Stories about Coffee

Mario Hernandez, a coffee farmer in Nicaragua, explains the difference between unfair and fair trade:

Beforehand we were paid by the middlemen who paid us whatever they felt like. Now the price is steady. If we are paid very little for a product we have nothing to buy food with. If you invest your money in the farm you have nothing left for food. Now I have money to buy my little children their little clothes. I could build my house. Day to day things are improving and this is because of the better price. Before, if we were ill all we had was a prescription but not the money to buy medicine. Now as we get better prices for our coffee we can have actual medicine not just a piece of paper. It is all a chain.

The co-operative sells to the Fair Trade coffee organization, Cafédirect.

Mario Hernandez
Nicaragua

The fair trade price makes it possible for us to invest in better methods of production and so to continually produce both better and organic coffee. And the more coffee we can produce under fair trade conditions the more money is left for us to support our families and to invest in the coffee plantations.

Robert Diaz Rivas
Peru

In Costa Rica both land and interest rates are very expensive. Small farmers, above all those who are very far off, often have to give up their land and move into the city to look for work and again that is very difficult. Thanks to Fair Trade it was possible for the coffee producers in Costa Rica to continue producing coffee and thus to ensure their existence.

Carlos A. Vargas
Costa Rica

Seventy-four-year-old Zacharia Kiwale, who has been a coffee farmer and member of his local co-op for many years, explains the impact coffee can have for an individual:

I built my house in 1973 when prices were good. I couldn't build such a house from coffee farming now. The trouble is that while coffee prices have hardly gone up since then – or even fallen sometimes – everything else has become much more expensive. When prices were better I was able to improve my farm – my coffee washing facilities were built in 1965 and I have another plot of land down the mountain where I grow maize and another where I grow rice.

Zacharia's 530 coffee trees produced 700 kg of coffee in 1995, worth $950. Income from coffee paid amongst other things for his grandchildren's school fees.

The people of Kilimanjaro are very development-orientated and we're all coffee farmers. As I look to the future, a better income for our coffee will mean better schools, better dispensaries and better roads . . . Currently all farmers have decided to contribute three shillings per kilo of coffee to our education fund which is worth approximately £30,000 per year. This is spent in twenty-two secondary schools to build classrooms and staff houses.

Zacharia Kiwale
Tanzania

Thank You God

Small producers have benefited
with Traidcraft. Better and
sustained incomes from fair
trade have brought real change
in the quality of life. The
enabling process has made for a
remarkable growth in skills.

But real growth for the
producers has been in the
intangibles, learning and
evolving, a sense of belonging
and togetherness.

Shabbi Kohli, Sasha (SSA)
India

Help Us Lord . . .

Help us Lord . . .
As we stand together . . .
for the ideals and practice of fair trade,
for the welfare of grassroots craft workers.

Help us Lord . . .
As we stand together . . .
against child labour,
against the exploitation of craft workers, farmers and
     growers.

Help us Lord . . .
As we stand together for fair business.

Moon Sharma, Tara Projects
India

Our Father Who is in Us

From Central America

Our Father
who is in us here on earth
holy is your name
in the hungry who share their bread and their song.
Your kingdom come,
a generous land where confidence and truth reign.
Let us do your will
being a cool breeze for those who sweat.
You are giving us our daily bread
When we manage to get back our lands
Or to get a fairer wage.

Forgive us
for keeping silent in the face of injustice
and for burying our dreams.
Don't let us fall into the temptation
of taking up the same arms as the enemy,
but deliver us from evil which disunites us.
And we shall have believed in humanity and in life
And we shall have known your kingdom
Which is being built for ever and ever.

Christian Aid

Praying for Change

Characters: Narrator (could also be the voice of God at the
end)
Miss Potts   Phyllis   Mrs Almond
Mr Rafferty   Rosie   Mario   Janeth

Setting   Church prayer group. Miss P, Mrs A, and Mr R
sitting in circle. Tables and chairs nearby.

Props　　　　　Tea and coffee containers – one side with fairly traded packaging, the other with the words TEA and COFFEE. Kettle, cups all on a tray. Bicycle (if possible).

Narrator　　　Let me introduce you to the church prayer group. They meet every week without fail to make sure that God is aware of the mess that his world is in. But, sshh, it's almost half past. Time for Miss Potts to lead the closing prayer.

Miss Potts　　Lord, you know that we long to see your justice and peace reign in the world. Please touch the hearts of all those who can make a difference. Amen.

Prayer Group Amen.

Miss Potts　　Right, folks. This church doesn't get any warmer does it? Just as well Phyllis has the kettle ready for a cup of something nice and hot.

(They move from the circle to a nearby table with chairs around it. Each sits down. Phyllis brings over a tray with kettle, jug, mugs plus a jar of coffee and a box of tea. She begins making drinks and distributing them).

Mr Rafferty　It's a terrible situation, isn't it. Watched it on the news last night. Dreadful. All those people suffering. If only we could do something.

Mrs Almond　But we can! Let's organize a jumble sale. Of course, we can't do that for a few weeks because we've got the concert in aid of the homeless coming up–

138

Miss Potts   And the church coffee morning. Don't forget our roof fund.

Mr Rafferty   Lord only knows how we'll ever manage to help them then.

(*Roll of drums/cymbal marks entrance of Rosie*)

Rosie   He certainly does!

(*Everyone stares at her*)

Mrs Almond   What do you mean?

Rosie   Didn't you say it in your prayers? Somewhere near the beginning I think . . . ah yes, that nice bit where you were praising God All-seeing, I think you called him.

Miss Potts   (*looking coy*) Oh, that was me. I'm glad it went down well.

Mr Rafferty   Just a minute. How do you know what we were saying? Were you hanging around outside?

Rosie   Don't worry about that. I'm not going to stay long. It's just that you made a request and I've come to help you.

Miss Potts   Request? I've never met you before in my life. We certainly didn't request that you came along – not that we're an exclusive group, you know. We're quite welcoming, it's just that no-one new ever comes to join us.

Rosie   Please touch the hearts of all those who can make a difference. Isn't that what you prayed?

(*The others look mystified, but nod*) Well I've come to tell you that you have made a difference! And I've brought my friend Mario to tell you how.

(*Mario walks on, stands by Rosie*)

He's a coffee farmer in Nicaragua and because your church drinks fairly traded tea and coffee, he wants to let you know the difference that you've made to the lives of him and his family.

Mrs Almond *Starting to look disconcerted, edges towards the coffee and tea jars so that she's standing in front of them*)

Well, we did try some coffee, Nicaraguan wasn't it? That must have been in Rev. Blaithwaite's time.

Mr Rafferty Yes, he was always very keen on this fair trade issue, wasn't he? But when he left we didn't hear much about it.

Miss Potts But we're eager to help with overseas charities and we have at least four fund-raising efforts a year and . . . (*Her voice trails away as Mario begins to speak*)

Mario Beforehand, we were paid by the middlemen who paid us whatever they felt like. Now the price is steady. If we are paid very little for a product we have nothing to buy food with. Now I have money to buy my little children their little clothes. I could build my house. Day to day things are improving and this is because of the better price.

140

Mr Rafferty   Sorry, but I can't help you. I can't stand coffee. Tea's my tipple. Well, before sunset anyway so–

Rosie   That's fine. Then meet my friend, Janeth.

(*Janeth walks on pushing a bicycle*)

Janeth   Working with Kibena Tea has enabled me to support my life with my family. Though I don't have my own house yet, I've been able to buy a bicycle, school my children, pay for fees and exercise books.

Mrs Almond   (*whispering to Phyllis*) Quick, hide the packets. Don't let them see what we've been drinking.

Rosie   So you see, he just wanted you to know that your prayers really do make a difference just like the tea and coffee you drink at the end of your meeting.

Miss Potts   But we're a small church. We drink what, half a dozen cups each meeting? How can that make a difference?

Rosie   But everyone's half a dozen cups of coffee adds up. That's more than three million cups of fairly traded coffee drunk in your country every week. It means a lot more people who can feed their families, provide homes, send their children to school. Your prayer meeting really does make a difference!

Mr Rafferty   (*whispering to Miss Potts*) This is terrible. (*He puts down the cup of tea he's been carrying*) Suddenly I'm not in the mood for this.

141

Rosie Well, I think I'll have a cup. All this travelling around makes me thirsty.

Miss Potts But I thought you'd want to drink fairly traded tea and coffee?

Rosie I do. (*Takes cup of tea from Phyllis*)

Mrs Almond Well, I'm afraid we drink this because we like the taste.

Rosie So do I. (*Takes a drink*)

Mr Rafferty What do you mean?

Rosie Go on, tell them, Phyllis.

(*Phyllis turns round the tea and coffee containers to show 'Teadirect' and 'Cafédirect'. The others gasp*)

Miss Potts But we don't like them!

Phyllis I changed over last year, when they had all those specials in the supermarket. No-one seemed to notice, except Mr Rafferty who said it was the best cuppa he'd had in ages.

Rosie How did your prayer go again?

Lord, you know that we long to see your justice and peace reign in the world. Please touch the hearts of all those who can make a difference.

Voice (God) Amen and thanks.

Traidcraft

Thoughts for Reflection

Our obsession with consumption means that we have become the future eaters, swallowing up the future of generations yet unborn.

Christ's third temptation was the temptation to acquire wealth and power ('all the kingdoms of the world', Matthew 4:8, 9). A contemporary example of the same temptation is rampant consumerism, regardless of the cost to other nations, future generations or to the earth itself.

If you have found all things within, you will not seek to accumulate all things without. To see poverty in our riches and riches in our poverty is a transforming awareness.

William L. Wallace
Aotearoa New Zealand

Favela, My Treasure

Favela*, my treasure
Your charm seduces me
With no water or electricity, you are
Still made of light
You're my inspirational muse my
Place, my land.
Hold tight, Favela,
Things are gonna get better.

Christian Aid
Brazil

* slum

Generous Hands

These hands do a lot of work.
Look at my generous hands
Look with care.
You can see the marks of my work
See the strength
See the pain.
This is how I live.
This is what my hands give.
Show me your hands;
Your hands are generous too.
Look with care.
What is your work, your strength,
Your pain?
How do you live?
What do your hands give?

Christian Aid
Haiti

The Test of Our Progress

The test of our progress is not whether we add more to the abundance of those who have much; it is whether we provide enough for those who have little.

Franklin D. Roosevelt

Open our eyes, just and loving God,
to the gross inequalities our privilege has created,
and give us courage to renounce the claim
to a super-abundance which extracts too much of the earth's
    resources.
Help us to see the connection between living in harmony
    with the natural world
and sharing its bounty with others.

May the people and the governments of the wealthy North
be inspired to make the quantum leap
that will be needed to apply the Roosevelt principle to the
   whole world.

Alan Litherland

Change My Destiny

If I could change my destiny
I wouldn't be a wanderer in
This harsh world.

As a good kid who worked in
The market, selling lemons
To earn his daily bread
I didn't repeat the cruelties I
Learned from life.
I can feed myself without
Robbing anyone.
I swear I didn't belong in those
Infamous orphanages
Where I lived since I was a
Baby.
It's hard to wake up at dawn to
Sell candy in the train.
If I could change my destiny I
Would be somebody,
But since I wasn't lucky enough
To get a good education
Today I'm called a punk and no
One gives me moral support.
If I had an option I wouldn't be
A social problem.

Christian Aid
Brazil

Some of Us

Some of us rush about,
spend moments we can count on our fingers
in our hi-tech kitchen,
slapping TV dinners into the microwave:
the 'soap'
or the 'web'
calls, and promptly glues us to the screen for hours
in a world of our own excess—
on our own in the world.

Some of us in a measured way,
bodies wearied by the labour of a long day,
cooking tasks allotted across the generations:
it's the dark-end of the day, 'catch-up' time—
banter, chatter, arguments, orders
crowd the air in the one room,
a world away—
so many, too many, only
subsist.

Some of us say,
God says:
'Share.'

Pamela Turner

Christ Our Advocate

Christ our Advocate,
we pray for our sisters and brothers throughout the world:
    out of our poverty and theirs,
    may we not stumble
    by judging each other.

Christ, brother of the poor,
in the faces of our partners may we see your love.
> In our faces may they see your love.
> Together may we abide in you,
> celebrating the risen life of the Kingdom.

Christ, bridge-builder,
help us to work with you and for you.
Through the power of the Spirit
> help us to rebuild God's community of divine purpose
> in partnership with all your people.

Kate McIlhagga

Crumbs of Cake

Crumbs of cake, that's all I've ever had, the leftovers,
The cast-offs and the hand-me-downs.
God, I'm desperately hungry for the cake,
A portion, a slice, on a plate at your table.

Crumbs of cake for me who's never had a chance,
Who's sat at people's feet and been treated like a dog.
God, I'm desperate for a feast of food,
The best of wine, the best of meat and seated as your guest.

Crumbs of cake have barely kept me living,
How I've survived I'll never know.
God, I'm desperate to be full and festive,
The best of celebrations, the new wine of the kingdom.

Crumbs of cake, that's all I've ever known.
I'm dirty and in rags and nobody's invited me.
God, I'm desperate and have nothing fit to wear.
Clothe me with your finest clothes, show me to my place.

Crumbs of cake, that poverty of life no more,
An abundance of your portions, a spread of excellence.
God, I'm desperately satisfied, filled with all good things,
As the richness of your banquet is lavished all on me.

Frances Ballantyne

I'm in Need

I'm thirsty and nobody knows
I'm hungry and nobody cares
I'm lonely and nobody comes
I'm crying and nobody hears
I'm dying and nobody notices.

I watch, seeing people pass me by.
I sit, hoping for someone to stop.
I despair, realizing I am alone.
I fall down, face down in the grime.
I lose awareness, out of human reach.

So helpless, when Jesus comes to help.
So weak, when Jesus holds me up.
So weary, when Jesus comforts me.
So powerless, when Jesus gives me strength.
So lifeless, when Jesus offers me his life.

So everybody, those who didn't see
So everybody, those who didn't care
So everybody, those who showed disgust
So everybody, those who walked away
So everybody, Jesus is my friend.

Frances Ballantyne

Fair Measure

God of the just weight
and the fair measure,
let me remember the hands
that harvested my food,
     my drink,
not only in my prayers
but in the market place.
Let me not seek a bargain
that leaves another hungry.

Janet Morley
Christian Aid

Harvest Prayer

Loving God,
great Creator,
we come with gratitude and praise
for all that is rich and wonderful in human life;
and with our bewilderment
over all that spoils it.

We come giving thanks
for the earth's resources,
and with our prayers
that the earth may not be desecrated
by human carelessness and greed;
and that the time may quickly come
when all the children of the world
will have all the food they need,
to grow up strong and healthy,
and to realize their infinite value
as your daughters and sons.

As we pray and praise you,
make us your answer to the prayers of Jesus.
Amen.

Alan Gaunt

Divine Redeemer

Divine Redeemer,
you long for your people to forgive
as you forgive
to share as bountifully
as you have so generously showered us with gifts.
Inspire us to open our hands;
to give as we have received.
May the rich nations of the north
be ready to forgive the debts
of the poorest nations of the south.
May we have the vision to go further
in reforming our global economic system
so that there is fair trading,
giving equal opportunities to all
and preventing heavy burdens of debt for the poor.
Help us each to have at heart
the welfare of all, old and young,
north and south, black and white,
so that your name may be honoured in our common life.

John Johansen-Berg

Inside Out

Black, white and gold
Are the colours of life—

For sorrow is black;
And the small seed of kindness
Unseen;

And the velvet of night
That hides love . . .

And the colour of skin.

For whiteness is pure;
And the breathless potential
Of dawn
Is revealed in the light
That hides nothing . . .

And the colour of skin.

For gold is of joy;
And the shining of sunlight
Unspent;
And the heat of the fire
That heals all . . .

And the colour of skin.

If the colours of life
Are the colours of skin—
Which clothes and encloses
The essence within—

Then the blood and the tears
Are the same.

Margot Arthurton

Lord of Life

Living Lord in our local community, focus our thoughts on
our many friends and neighbours who support practical
action for people who have no local harvest whether from
field or industry.

Thank you for the produce displayed which reflects our local community.

Thank you for the people who are involved with selling and purchasing Fair Trade items and for the supermarkets which respond to campaigns to stock these items on their shelves.

Living Lord in our wider community, focus our thoughts on the drought-prone areas of south India (*or name another place*).

Thank you for the different religions and cultures working together for good. Thank you for the village people who are resilient and resourceful. When the rains do not fall their crops fail; when the rains falls in ceaseless torrent the crops that have grown are flooded and harvesting cannot take place.

Bless them in their smiling and their laughing in the face of disaster, especially when women and men migrate to the cities but find no work.

Bless us, Lord of Life.
Protect us from complacency.
Bless us, Lord of the harvest season.
Encourage us to accept challenges,
to take risks for people less fortunate than ourselves
and to have the courage to be in solidarity with people
who need your love given
through us.
Amen.

Geoffrey Duncan

One Family

People come and go in the market place;
they see others in different hues;
here there are black and white, indigenous and immigrant,
a rainbow people but truly together,
a people of one family.
We seek to bear each other's burdens;

we seek to share each other's joys;
we share our happiness and our sorrows;
why then do some seek to make us enemies?
We are one family, God's people,
a rainbow people whose song is love.

Responsive Prayer:

Leader: Give strength to hands that are tired.
Tell everyone who is discouraged,

Response: **Be strong and do not be afraid:**
God is coming to rescue you.

Leader: For the people who leave a land of poverty
seeking assured food for their children,

Response: **Do not be discouraged: God is with you.**

Leader: For people who flee from oppression
seeking freedom in a far land,

Response: **Do not be discouraged: God is with you.**

Leader: For those who have come to a strange country
and find themselves subject to insult and
discrimination,

Response: **Do not be discouraged: God is with you.**

Leader: For those who offer their gifts in the community
and find that they are rejected,

Response: **Do not be discouraged: God is with you.**

Leader: Tell everyone who is hurt and fearful,
be strong and do not be afraid.

Response: God is with you; you will see his love and
power.

What gives us our unity and strength?
It is the law which gives to each
rights upheld by courts.
What gives us our unity and trust?
It is the social contract which gives to each
rights and responsibilities.
What gives us our unity and peace?
It is the covenant-offering to all from each,
a compassionate relationship of love.

John Johansen-Berg

The Multi-Grain Bread of Life

Seven streetkids – bare feet and bad attitudes
Disarmingly cute, alarmingly tough. Boys.
The youngest – who looks no older than six – doesn't smile.
They are a badge of courage for the middle-class
    congregation
who have ventured into the not so safe centre of Joburg
on a cold Sunday night.
No-one knows how to reach them – we cannot touch their
    world.

Church. First singing then prayer, sermon,
and communion.
The streetkids confidently approach the communion rail
to take the bread and drink from the cup.
Impatiently they kneel there. Sticking fingers into small
    cup-sized holes.
Then grubby hands reach up
correctly cupped, outstretched, waiting to be filled
with the bread of Life.

Hardly – just a small piece of multi-grain sliced bread
the crust still on.
The bread of everyday life – for us
not for them.
A thimble full of grape juice, glasses licked with eager
    tongues.
Then – that's it.

One young opportunist stays at the rail
with his grubby cupped hands outstretched. Hoping for more
crumbs from the Lord's table.
The minister obliges, offering a second helping of the
Body of Christ – given for you – and His blood
Shed for you – for you – and for you.
All the boys have come back
for seconds.
Take and eat.

Finally, when the elements are exhausted
the street children are told
It is finished.
Go back to your seats. Reluctantly they go.
The small boy with the grubby hands is gently picked up
and carried away from the rail. His hands
cupped, outstretched,
looking up at the steward with hungry eyes that would
    break
your heart.

Let us finish with prayer
for the hungry.

Afterwards, one prepared saint
brings loaves of bread for the children.

The young pastor, who knows of heartbreak
in this cruel city, watches them go – into the night.

'We must respect communion,' he says to no-one in
    particular,
but we must also respect their hunger.'
No-one in particular was listening.

Jeff Thompson
South Africa

All You Have Given

Based on Philippians 4:4–20; 1 Peter 4:7–11

All you have given calls us, Lord, to praise you–
Abundant wealth through Jesus Christ our Lord–
Your peace to guard our hearts in times of trouble;
Our needs supplied, our broken strength restored.

Teach us to use your varied gifts with wisdom,
Sharing with others for the good of all;
May we delight in giving and receiving,
And hold each other up, that none may fall.

To you, our God and Father, be the glory,
For in all things the praise belongs to you;
We pledge our thankful service to your people,
That we may show your love through what we do.

Tune: Highwood

Jenny Dann

Enslaved by Debt, a Worldwide Grief

Enslaved by debt, a worldwide grief
Cries out through pain for liberty;
The chains that bound us in the past
Ensure today's captivity.

156

Our greed for wealth, our selfishness,
Will hold us in our apathy,
And others starve and die because
We have no mutual sympathy.

Enslaved by fear, we need to risk
The loss that others ought to gain
That, from self-sacrificial love,
New joy may grow from seeds of pain.

Then from this season's hopelessness
Help us to set each other free;
And when our only debt is love,
Lord, share our joy at jubilee.

Andrew Pratt

Give Us This Day

In this day, give us your strength,
Enough to last the day.
In work and play, in rest and sleep,
Enough to last the day.

Supply and feed us in our need.

Give us today our daily bread,
Enough to last the day.
The manna for our bodies, strength,
Enough to last the day.

Supplying, satisfying and full.

Frances Ballantyne

The Dawning of Another Day

With the beckoning and dawning of another day,
can the fragile, yet extraordinary
words of Jesus
propel us to a wider awareness
a gentler compassion?
To the rediscovery of the sacred in ourselves,
and in our world?
To that risk-taking place
where the imprisoning bonds
of our self-enclosed lives are finally shattered?
To a different journey
in a listening companionship
with the prophets of our time—
the wounded and weary
who announce the kingdom
and carry in their stories the seeds of the morrow?
The 'hidden ones'
in our global culture,
whose pain and joy
when threaded through our lives
enlarge the heart
and bring new meaning
to our common future:
that sacred future
where, impossible as it may seem,
we 'love our neighbours as ourselves'.

Peter Millar

Part Five:

Summer and winter, and springtime and harvest . . .

'As long as the earth endures, seedtime and harvest, cold and heat, summer and winter, day and night shall not cease.'
Genesis 8:22

Harvest Reflection

At harvest we thank God for all his gifts of food and weather, especially his plants which mature in autumn and nourish us all year. Harvest is also an opportunity to give thanks and to praise God for all creatures which move in the waters, fly in the sky and live on the land. Harvest reminds us that all earth's creatures are a community created to praise and glorify God. Nature matures in autumn even without human help. Wild creatures enjoy the fruits of the season. With human co-operation, however, nature glorifies God through cultivated fields, including grain and grapes which make bread and wine. Human hands and voices represent the whole earth community, in Christ, to God. The transformation of the earth at harvest is a sign, the beginning of the final transformation of all material creation in the resurrection when God does not make a new thing, but makes 'all things new'.

Edward P. Echlin

Put People before Profit

The following two stories are to be read in association with the prayer which follows:

Hope Ndyaboneka

Hope Ndyaboneka is a widow with a family to support.

'There has been a drastic fall of income on my sweet potatoes, coffee, bananas and beans. Our poverty is getting worse. Trade liberalization in Uganda was hurried and has not helped us here in Bitooma Parish. I mobilize other coffee growers to build our co-operative. That's all I can do.'

Ngambe Eliab

Ngambe Eliab is from the village of Igambiro. He grows coffee, bananas, beans and millet to support his family – there are twelve in all. There is no access to market information so middlemen can pay them low prices. They operate on behalf of the big multinational coffee buyers. He is part of the Katenge Omunjoki farm co-op which supports Fair Trade – it pays a good price and Ngambe is campaigning for quality improvement for the coffee crops so that they can sell more to the Fair Trade market.

World Development Movement

Leader: Harvest God,
encourage us to be better educated
about the immense diversity
of basic, staple foods for health and well-being
which need to be grown around the world;
the livelihoods which depend
on the various forms of farming;
the families who need practical support.

Response: **In our hearts, Harvest God,
we know that we must put people before profit.**

Leader: God of the coffee farmer,
encourage us to be better educated
about the local farmers and their families
and the co-operatives where coffee is grown,
so that the poverty of these communities
causing threats to health
becomes better known in our small part of your
world.

Response: **In our hearts, God of the coffee farmer,**
we know that we must put people before profit.

Leader: God of the fruit farmer,
encourage us to be better educated
about the dependency of families
on the fruits of their farming;
the oranges and apples
bananas and guavas
mangoes and melons
which we examine and select
as we purchase for the week
or stock up for the next Bank Holiday.

Response: **In our hearts, God of the fruit farmer,**
we know that we must put people before profit.

God, in our selective thinking
Christ in your compassion
Spirit of perseverance
enlighten our God-given minds to the
immense, basic needs of
women and men in struggling
communities,
enable us to turn over the tables in the
temples of greed
and to become the radical people of
Christ,
encourage us to speak and act through
the power of the Spirit.

Response: **In our hearts, Harvest God,**
we know that we must put people before profit.

Geoffrey Duncan

You are the Life of the World

We pray for the rain,
the wind of the sky,
the fruit of the earth,
the fruit of the trees and of the vineyards.
Bring them up according to their measure
that they may grow and prosper through your grace.
Make the face of the earth to rejoice,
water her furrows,
let her grain be abundantly multiplied
and make ready her seed time and her harvest.
You are life for our souls.
You are the life of the world.

Let your hand rest upon your people,
widows and orphans, aged and children,
strangers and wanderers.
And join us also with them,
protect and strengthen us,
from all evil works keep us apart,
and in all good works unite us.
You are life for our souls.
You are the life of the world.

Ethiopian Orthodox Church

Thoughts on an Early Morning Walk in Central Java

God spoke
and His words
took form and colour
light shone
water roared
seed sprang to life
earth burst forth
from bud to blossom

and the first bird
sang.
God breathed
and dust became
a man and with him
woman.

I walked and I heard
a voice breathe
in the live earth
green-growing
slopes with square
of rice padi layer
on layer filled
with water flowing
from step
to step.

Women, backs bent
knee deep, intent
on planting.
I watched them—
words God spoke
took flesh form
and colour and
in the sunshine
moved.

And as I bend
to the earth
I know
His seed gives Life,
His every word
a song.

Pamela Ferguson

Mr Vasappa

Medak District in Andra Pradesh, south India, is dry and barren. Dirt tracks and the occasional tarmac road dissect dusty fields of crops of grasses but mostly there are great expanses of thirsty, rocky soils dotted with the occasional coarse bush tree and large patches of red, open soil through which gullies have been carved by seasonal rains, like bleeding wounds on the rugged landscape. Centuries ago these lands would have been forested but now very few trees remain and the area resembles a moonscape.

Recent agricultural practices have not helped. The government has subsidized pesticides and irrigation schemes in order to promote sugar cane farming to supply its local sugar mill. More land for cotton growing is likely to be made available. Both cash crops require intensive agricultural techniques which use a great deal of water, lowering the water table and leaving the soil exposed for certain periods which leads to severe erosion.

The Deccan Development Society (DDS) has assisted schemes to develop large areas of wasteland around villages by removing rocks and planting hardy trees. Hundreds of villagers have been involved in growing certain medicinal crops and herbs in an attempt to reclaim some of the lost traditional remedies. Women have been involved in environmental campaigning and marching in protest against cotton growing and its impact.

With the help of DDS, Mr Vasappa dug an open well, fifteen feet deep, to supply water for irrigation for a small farm he was establishing. Since then he has had to remove thousands of small red rocks which now form chest-high walls around his plots in order to leave a little workable soil. He grows all kinds of produce from mulberries to sorghum. He supplies papaya to the local *balwadis* (nursery schools) in the district and acts as a local garden centre where mango saplings and other hardy plants are grown for distribution to farmers who are committed to re-forestation. The water from his well irrigates twenty-two acres of land that is farmed by a *sangham* of forty-four women.

Mr Vasappa has rarely left his farm. In fact, when his daughter was married in Hyderabad he told her he would not be making the journey. 'If I come,' he said, 'all my trees will get lonely.'

Edward Cox

Staple Diet in Ethiopia

Meals in Ethiopia are a time of sharing and giving. One of the most popular dishes is *wo'ts* which is a stew. It is usually served on a giant pancake called *injera*. *Wo'ts* can also be served with rice, bread, salads, humous and dhals.

Injera pancakes are a tasty part of the staple for Ethiopian people.

Our Prayer

> Let us pray
> for the people of Ethiopia
> for the well-fed and the hungry
> for the strong and the weak
> for the lands without rain where little grows.
>
> Let us pray
> for the churches of Ethiopia
> as they share Christ's suffering and love,
> struggle to feed their people,
> call to us for help;
> and for these our churches
> as we hear their cry.
>
> Let us pray for ourselves
> and the part we can play
> in the journey from hunger and distress
> to needs well met by a fruitful earth.

Source Unknown

Bangladeshi Farmers

Bangladeshi farmers are busy all year round. Many more are farm-hands having smallholdings, where they need strong muscles, others have no land at all. Some are share-croppers. Too many are land-labourers. They know well how to plough with bullocks, how to sow seed and harvest all round the year. There is the rainy season and there was the time for harvesting pulses and linseed. However, these crops have disappeared from the land as the special rice crops have taken over.

Whilst the low delta land is empty the higher grounds have three rice crops of three months duration for each one. It is called IRRI after the name of the International Rice Research Institute, Philippines which is sponsored by the Bangladesh, Joydevpur BIRRI Institute. There has been continuous development of new, genetically engineered, disease resistant and high yielding varieties of rice; improved varieties called Alo (light) have even come across the border from India and yields have multiplied. We are told that some special varieties will need special seeds to be procured not from our own rice products but from some companies that continue to develop it.

Much more is required than these products to feed so many hungry people. The present development vocabulary is 'food-security' – sometimes one fails to understand how to secure food for those millions of landless and penniless people. How are they to avoid living hand to mouth even when the rice is being harvested, when the share for the landless is very small?

It is not enough for beyond two or three months. Where there is one crop only it may be enough for the rich land-owning people. Where there are three harvests in higher areas, often the north and west of the country, it is better for the poor to survive and there is some security of food.

How long shall we go on exploiting the land, Mother Earth, using all kinds of chemical fertilizers and insecticides so that the harvest will increase many-fold? The water gets polluted by iron from the tube-wells and the eco-cycle is destroyed. We need a green revolution so that there will be many-fold returns to feed the millions. In this scarcity of food there cannot be any rest for the farm-hands, for the landless – we need plentiful harvests.

Bishop Barnabas Dwijen Mondal
Bangladesh

Seedlings

There is a very simple and meaningful practice among the woefully underpaid farm labourers of Tamil Nadu, south India.

Rice is the staple food for the people of Tamil Nadu state. The seed form of rice with its husk is called paddy. Paddy is cultivated in wet fields. It is first sown thickly in a small plot of land. The seedlings are then transplanted in well-spaced rows in another larger field made wet and muddy.

Girls from the families of those at work will go to the road and nearby streets with small bunches of seedlings in their hands. They will place them at the feet of the passers-by, and with the left hand pointing to the fields where the work is in progress will stretch out the right hand and ask for a small donation. Many people will give a few coins, often cursing the urchins for resorting to begging: the real meaning of this 'begging' has eluded them.

The meaning, however, was made known by one young girl. A passer-by scolded her for taking to begging. She faced him courageously and retorted that she was not a beggar. She asked the man to look at the fields where many women were standing in a bent posture in ankle deep wet mud, involved in transplanting the seedlings. She then told the man that they were working in order that he could be fed and sustained. Having thus made the man aware of his heavy indebtedness to these people who were so poorly paid, she then demanded with great dignity that he give her a handsome donation.

The challenge to remember all the underpaid and unpaid

labour with a grateful heart is great – and was indeed the reason behind the practice.

Bread is made of God's gifts in nature – rain, fertility of soil and seed. But it is also made with human labour. The sweat of toil is a constituent element of bread. Our Lord seems to have wanted people, in the Eucharist, to become aware how, in ordinary bread, God and human labour were united in a process of self-giving to sustain life.

Dhyanchand Carr
India

Spreading Hope

Risen Lord of the harvest,
as the wild flower scatters its seeds far and wide,
so may your people scatter the seed of hope
in the soils of despair
bringing to growth those good things
that are your gift and promise.

Christopher P. Burkett

Hear Our Prayer

We pray for farmers,
their families and communities
and all who depend on them.
Lord, in your mercy,
Hear our prayer.

For agricultural chaplains,
support groups
and rural churches,
Lord, in your mercy,
Hear our prayer.

170

For restraint and fairness in the use of economic power,
For discernment and a long view in policy and decision,
For love of creation in farm policy and practice,
For justice in world trade,
Lord, in your mercy,
Hear our prayer.

For ourselves that we may eat
with joy and with care;
For land and livestock
and love for those who care for them,
Lord, in your mercy,
Hear our prayer.

The Arthur Rank Centre

Terminology

Productivity:
Forced outcome of
Endeavour;

Unlike *fruitfulness:*
Result of fallow
Darkness
When time seems wasted.

Seasons take their time:
Nothing is lost, our waiting,
Open and expectant
Leads to harvest.

Ann Lewin

Summer's End

Swooping swallows,
long, light nights,
laughing children:
    reward-sure weariness trudges home,
    hay bales high,
    weather dry,
    combine quiet.

Raucous crows,
fast-blanketing dark,
stick-thin, large-eyed children:
    resigned, staring fear trudges home,
    effort in vain,
    withered, scarce grain,
    bullock dead.

Pamela Turner

Autumnal God

O Autumnal God, splendour of rainbow hued leaves, may
the eventide of our lives be a vibrant prelude to the all-
encompassing letting go of death.

William L. Wallace
Aotearoa New Zealand

Autumn Leaf

This autumn
shall be for me
the most glorious
of them all
for I shall no longer
struggle possessively
to clutch life
but instead

172

like a leaf
let myself
be blown
by God's Spirit
and whenever
I touch the earth
sing the song of the universe
dance in the power of God's grace
and with tenderness
offer myself
to all.

William L. Wallace
Aotearoa New Zealand

The Celebration of Harvest is a Celebration of the Cycle of Life

Leader: God of Life,
We live in your world with its seasons and cycles.
Day by day you nurture the life within us carefully encouraging growth,
that we might bloom where we are planted and produce a rich harvest from our lives.

Response: Life-giving God, grow in us.

Leader: God of the Harvest,
At harvest time, help us to celebrate the letting go,
keeping only what's needed to sow the next crop.
in the fallow time that follows, allow us time
for dreaming about what might be and to prepare the fertile soil of our minds.

Response: **God of the Harvest, help us to let go.**

Leader: God of New Life,
Plant new seed within us
and work your resurrection miracle
as you bring again new signs of life.
Let your quiet energy flow through our
being,
working unseen, growing new ideas and
new ways.

Response: **God of New Life, let your energy flow through us.**

All: **Living God, help us to celebrate the cycle of life with us,
and the harvest it brings.
Amen**

The Uniting Church in Australia

The Cycles of Nature

Interwoven web of life
holding as one
stream and song,
sinew and silence,
seedtime and harvest,
how I delight in you
and you in me.
You are the universal face of God
the touch of true divinity,
the infusion and expansion,
the beyond and the within,
the growing and the dying,
the separation and the merging.

174

In you the threads are woven,
the sea surges,
the sun shines
and the earth nurtures.
Alleluia   Alleluia   Alleluia

William L. Wallace
Aotearoa New Zealand

A Paraphrase of Ecclesiastes 3:1–8

There is a time for everything in creation
  a time for light and a time for darkness,
  a time for sound and a time for silence,
  a time for action and a time for reflection,
  a time for work and a time for play,
  a time for waking and a time for sleep,
  a time for holding on and a time to let go,
  a time for death and a time for new beginnings.

There is a time for negotiation and a time for confrontation
  a time for advance and a time for retreat,
  a time for laughter and a time for tears,
  a time for intimacy and a time for solitude,
  a time for others and a time for oneself.

But all these times are God's time
and now is the time to be aware.

William L. Wallace
Aotearoa New Zealand

At the Drop of Rain God Visits Us

At the drop of rain God visits us
We all sow our seeds in our gardens
Trees are beautifully dressed in green
Fruits appear on the trees again
We are assured of bumper food harvest.

At the drop of rain God visits us
Grass for thatching our houses becomes taller again
Cattle and wildlife graze on fresh grass and tender leaves
All wells and springs in the village become full again
We all become excited and children dance.

At the drop of rain God visits us
Drought becomes a thing of the past
Our storehouses become full with food items
Our agro-based economy boosts again
Our bodies look healthy again.

When the rain suddenly stops we feel the absence of God
Drought appears on the scene
We fall into the vicious cycle of hunger again
Our faces look miserable and hopeless
We lack food to feed our empty stomachs.

When the rain suddenly stops
Prices of food commodities go higher
Our economy suffers and inflation becomes a new song
Cattle and wildlife terribly suffer
As pasture for grazing dries up.

At the drop of the rain God visits us
And we thank God for the harvests.

But when the rain suddenly stops
We pray to God who always identifies with us.

Goodwin Zainga
Malawi

Worship for a Worldwide Harvest

The piece is written for five characters: a Leader; Voices One and Two who are friends talking; Three and Four who are commentators.

Leader: Let us worship God.

Reading: Genesis 4:9

One: We are our brothers' and sisters' keepers.
Two: We are all one.
Three: We share a common humanity.
Four: We share a common world.

Hymn: Now join we to praise the creator.

Leader: Father, we gather to praise you and to give you thanks for the good things in our lives.

You are the Lord of this world and of all it contains – the Lord of all harvests. We thank you that you let us share in the world's bounty; but we admit our sin and failure because so many do not.

You made us stewards of your creation, to care for it and make this world and all that is in it hymn your praise; but we admit our sin and failure because so much of what was beautiful we have despoiled and destroyed.

You made all men and women in your image, to be one family of the same parent. We thank you for the joys of human love and fellowship; but we admit our sin and failure shown by the contempt and violence that we see around us.

Lord, forgive us what is wrong in our lives and our world and help us to change. Amen.

One:	We are one in you and in each other.
Two:	Help us to remember that our actions affect others in this country and on the other side of the globe;
Three:	Help us to remember that our attitudes affect others in this country and on the other side of the globe;
Four:	And help us also to remember that the hopes, attitudes and responsibilities of those others elsewhere in this world are just as valid and important as our own.

Reading: Deuteronomy 16:13–14

Two:	Did you have a nice holiday?
One:	Oh yes! Africa's wonderful and the people seem so happy. We went on a trip to see a farming village. It was really nice. They were much more in tune with things than we are. But I was reading that it's all having to change because of supermarkets.
Two:	Supermarkets? Have they got them in Africa?
One:	No – well yes – but I mean our supermarkets. Apparently all these farmers are being forced to grow things for Freshco instead of things for their families.
Two:	That's terrible.
Three:	Is it? Surely it's subsistence farming that's terrible. If you're a subsistence farmer you can't grow refrigerators or washing powder, you can't grow medical treatment or education for your children. Your diet is boring and lacks vital food value because you can only grow a few things. Growing cash crops gives farmers choice.
Four:	What is terrible is the fact that producers often don't get a fair exchange for their labour. Our shops now stock organic produce. They will also stock fairly traded produce if we take the trouble to ask and keep on asking and buy it when it's available.
Leader:	Father, help us to see that our supermarkets pay a

fair price for the crops farmers grow. Rather than ask others to make sacrifices let us be prepared to pay realistic prices for their labour. Amen.

Silence or open prayer

Leader: Lord in your mercy . . .
All: **Hear our prayer**

Fairly traded products are placed on the harvest table

Hymn: For the fruits of his creation

Reading: Isaiah 2:4

One: Did you see the news about America?
              There's been another shooting.
Two: Another one? That's terrible. They should stop letting people have guns.
One: That's what I say. It's not right to make money out of giving people the means to kill each other.
Three: It's not. But the UK is one of the biggest exporters of arms in the world. If we say it is wrong to sell guns to individuals, is it right to sell guns to governments?
Four: Of course we try to make sure only friendly governments are our customers.
Three: But governments change. British arms have been used by many repressive regimes.
Four: Yet if we don't sell them small countries won't have the means to defend themselves. They can't manufacture their own.
Leader: Lord, give us wisdom to decide these difficult questions. Help us to work towards a world where small countries no longer need to waste resources on arms. Where nation speaks peace unto nation. Amen.

Silence or open prayer

Leader: Lord in your mercy . . .
All: **Hear our prayer**

Model weapons and garden tools are placed on the harvest table

Hymn: Behold, the mountain of the Lord

Reading: Genesis 1:29–30

One: I was reading about genetically modified plants in the paper the other day.
Two: Oh, I don't hold with that. It's tampering with nature!
One: I didn't think I did, but they were saying that they could improve plants to prevent disease in people, or breed them to grow in places where they would normally not survive.
Two: What's the point of that? We've got medicines to cure people and there's plenty of food – grain mountains and wine lakes and I don't know what else.
One: I suppose you're right – but it seemed to make sense when I read it.
Two: If I had my way we'd grow everything in the old-fashioned way – organically, even if it did cost a bit more. The world would be a better place without all these artificial fertilizers and things.
Three: But we have a choice. We often have too much food and plenty of money.
Four: Dr Cyrus Ndirtu, director of the Kenyan Agricultural Research Institute, said: 'Its nice to be romantic about not using chemicals, not using fertilizers, not using gene technology. But just remember, for people in parts of rural Africa, Asia and Latin America, the choice is between life and death.'

Three: – And not about whether to pay a bit more in the supermarket for organic produce. If we wish to impose our principles on others who have so much less than we have, we must be prepared to meet the costs. It may be laudable for someone to die for their own principles; to ask someone else to die for those principles is not.

Leader: Father, give us a view of this world as truly one world. May we not ask of others sacrifices we would not make ourselves.

Silence or open prayer

Leader: In your mercy . . .
All: **Hear our prayer**

Symbols of science and finance are placed on the harvest table

Reading: Matthew 25:31–46.

(This reading may be split between four voices)

Leader: Lord, we live in one world. We are all brothers and
        sisters in you.
        Grant us the patience, persistence, wisdom and will
        to pay the cost of doing what is right. Amen.

Hymn: Praise God for the harvest of farm and field

Leader: Bless us, Lord, as we leave this place.
        Bless us in the produce of the earth
        And in the produce of human hands and minds.
        Bless us in the light that shines on us
        In the rain that falls on us
        And in your loving grace that goes with us. Amen.

Alan Bell

Gnarled Old Trees

Gnarled old trees
Lie broken
And dead,
Struck down in their prime,
No longer bearing fruit
Or growing
Through the cycle of the seasons.

Yet in their brokenness
Is beauty;
Weathered, hollowed out,
Timeless beauty.

They were meant to die.
For in their dying
They sustain the life of others.

A honeycomb
Grows deep inside the hollow,
Bringing sweetness to the brokenness.

Butterflies dance
Around the smoothly textured bark.

Lichens and mosses
Root in the crevices
Where once the sap did flow.

Heavenly blue dragonflies
Hover around about.

Beauty from brokenness . . .
Life from death . . .

Pat Marsh

Bread and Wine

Thank you, Lord,
For flour and yeast,
Risen dough,
Leavened life.

Thank you, Lord,
For wine to feast,
Fruitful harvest,
Love increased.

Thank you, Lord,
You came to the least,
Sins forgiven,
Spirit freed.

Lesley K. Steel

Harvest Gifts

Tune: Ode to Joy

Bring to God your gifts for harvest
celebrate God's love with praise!
God has filled the earth with good things
in their seasons, year by year:
field and forest, mine and ocean
yield their crop for all to share,
given for human life's enrichment,
tokens of our Maker's care.

Bring to God your gifts for harvest
celebrate God's love with praise!
Gifts of mind and hand and talent
echo God's creative power.
Human hands tend God's creation
body, mind and soul are fed.
Work and rest and worship offer—
at God's feet all may be laid.

183

Bring to God your gifts for harvest—
every day's activity!
Worship God in home and office
boardroom, classroom, factory.
Join the song of adoration,
join the symphony of praise.
Bring to God your gifts for harvest
bring the fruit of all your days.

Heather Pencavel

Pirouette

The beauty is as real as dust and sweat;
garden or living room as much a part
of life as turmoil. Toil's not all we get

through being here, though it's the portion set
if we're to perfect a thing, make of our art
the beauty that's as real as dust and sweat;

lasts, and is worth remembering. The net
we cast must take in both, the heavy heart
and joy of knowing toil's not all we get.

The bliss of autumn's breathing, pirouette
of apples under the thick leaves' rampart,
this beauty is as real as dust and sweat.

In travail and in loss we can't forget
the pulse of Spring, the stars by which we chart
the perilous course, prove toil's not all we get.

Nature and artefact do not regret
labour and love that form and set apart
the virtue in them. Toil's not all we get.
The beauty's real because of dust and sweat.

Brian Louis Pearce

Beans and Apples Grow Together

The Cherokees, who are among the most cultured of all the Native American communities, took some seeds with them when they were forcibly evicted from their homeland in 1838. The seeds were from the lovely pastel blue/green bean which is called the Cherokee Trail of Tears. Try to grow and then save the seeds of this climbing French bean.

The Cherokees sowed the beans at the base of sweetcorn, letting the plants climb and support themselves on the stalk. As a legume, the bean returned the favour by fixing nitrogen in the soil. I follow the Cherokees' example by sowing the seed near my upright cordon apples and plums. The beans use the tree for a ladder, enjoying the rainwater and compost I give the tree. After the autumn harvest I cut the beans off a few inches above the soil, leaving the roots to fix nitrogen.

So far both beans and fruit have flourished symbiotically, enjoying each other's gifts. The blue of the beans add beauty to the tree. People enjoy the slender beans mixed with the leaves and fruitlets and the ease of picking. Together the fruit and the bean contribute, as does all organic horticulture, to what G. K. Chesterton called 'the uproarious labour by which all things live'.

Growing rare beans with equally rare apples is admittedly a small-scale contribution to a local community. But if more of us live sustainably locally the amazingly small universe has a chance.

Edward P. Echlin

Life-Blood

What goes around
Comes around:
The cycle of the seasons
Throbs like a heart-beat,
Giving continuity and rhythm
To all of your Creation.

Creator God –
Pouring out your life-blood
Into the sap of trees,
The rains from heaven,
The waters of streams,
Rivers and seas.

Coursing through every capillary,
Vein and artery
Of your wondrous world.
Channelling your power
And your vital energy
To every part it is needed.

Susan Hardwick

Seasoned Creation

From the wintry white wastes
of the Arctic,
to the burning summer heat
of the Equator,
the seasons of the year
spice and flavour your Creation.

Wondrous God,
I picture the coolness
of your finger,
or the warmth of your touch,
according to what or where
you are shaping.

As with your world,
so it is with people,
of every shape and hue,
reflecting different aspects,
different shades of you.

186

Thank you,
Generous God,
for a world so rich
in its diversity.
and for a breadth of humankind
that constantly challenges
and stretches
our understanding of you.

Susan Hardwick

Seasons

A chant for a Primary School

*If a tune is not available the children need some space to move
rhythmically and shout out the words as if 'on the move'.*

As the Autumn leaves fall down,
red and yellow, green and brown;
we recall God loves us all
as the Autumn leaves do fall!

As the Winter trees all bare,
wave their branches in the air;
we remember all God's care
when the Winter trees are bare!

When the Spring leaves start to sprout
and the blossoms all come out;
welcome new life with a shout
when the Spring leaves start to sprout!

When the Summer trees do sway,
in the branches we can play;
we enjoy God's love all day,
when the Summer branches sway!

Janet Lees

Sower, Nurturer, Winnower

Glory to you, New Covenant Maker, sower of seeds,
for whom and through whom all things exist.
We thank you for recreating us.

Glory to you, Christ of the field, nurturer of seedlings,
pointing to the possibilities of growth.
We thank you for being with us.

Glory to you, Harvesting Spirit, winnower of husk and chaff,
blowing through our hopes for today.
We thank you for renewing us.

Glory to you, Holy Three, wholly one,
dancing together like thistledown on the wind.
We dance with you and celebrate your gift of life.

Janet Lees

From Season to Season

From season to season, through death to rebirth
this world, through its phases, shows love has no dearth.
This love is for sharing, to do good to all,
to nurture well-being, to echo God's call.

Through sensitive reason we fathom the need
of neighbours, of nature; we subjugate greed.
We offer each other the kiss of God's peace,
embracing earth's harmony, hatred will cease.

Through summer and autumn, through winter's release,
we welcome spring's coming with nature's increase.
All praise for the gifting of harvest and life,
all power to the ending of all human strife.

Andrew Pratt

A Harvest Communion Service

Invitation:

Take a seed . . .

A seed can be planted in some earth.

> Reap wheat from a field;
> take yeast from the earth;
> mix water from the well;
> break salt from the rock.
> Knead them together
> for the Bread of Life.

Take a seed . . .

A seed can be planted in some earth.

> Plant trees in the orchard;
> prune branches in the vineyard;
> pick good fruit from the vine;
> crush grapes into wine.
> Work them together
> for a drink to remember.

Take a seed . . .

A seed can be planted in some earth.

> Sow the word in your heart;
> reap peace from your weeping;
> share hope through your loving;
> harvest justice in your living.
> Mix them together
> for a Kingdom to come.

From the harvest in the field
God offers bread to break and share.

From the harvest of the vineyard
God offers grapes and wine to share.

From the harvest of human hearts
God offers love and peace to bring and share.

Through the Son who lived the Word
God invites you to come and share a harvest supper
from which no-one will be turned away.

Reflective Narrative:

Let us reflect on how the story of this sacrament began and
prepare our hearts and minds so that what we receive may
find good soil in which the seeds of the Kingdom can find
deep roots to grow and multiply:

On the night on which he was betrayed by one of his friends
Jesus sat at supper with his disciples and while they were eating took a piece of bread, said a blessing, broke it and gave it to
them saying: 'This is like my body which is broken for you. Do
this to remember me.'

So let us pause and reflect on what we should remember
before we break this bread:

We remember how you healed whether people's faith was
   great or small, and can do the same for us.
We remember the Good News you proclaimed for the poor
   and asked the rich to follow too.
We remember how you taught us to love neighbour, stranger,
   and give as much to our enemies.
We remember your life, how you resisted temptation, healed
   the sick, released the prisoners, gave sight to the blind, and
   asked us to do the same and follow you.

190

We remember how your life was broken for us, but you rose from death to offer new hope in the Kingdom to come.

Then, after supper, he took the cup, saying: 'This Cup is God's new covenant sealed with my love which is poured out for many for the forgiveness of sins. Drink from it, all of you to remember me.'

So let us pause again and reflect on how we have forgotten to live as Jesus taught us and how we need his healing forgiveness in our lives . . . *(time for quiet reflection)*

Blessing of Bread and Wine:

As the Word grew in Christ
  to become the Bread of Life
    which people took and broke,

So the seed sown in the soil
  became the wheat which makes the bread
    which we now break and ask the Holy Spirit to bless as
      we prepare to share.

As Jesus was the vine
  from which grew the fruits of love
    poured out for the healing of our lives,
So the seed sown in the soil
  became the tree, producing fruit crushed into wine
    which we now take and ask the Holy Spirit to bless as we
      prepare to share.

Thanksgiving Prayer:

Leader: Prepare your hearts
All: We prepare them for the Lord
Leader: Open your minds
All: We open them for the Word

Leader: Let us give thanks to the Lord our God

All: We give thanks for the goodness of creation

Leader: Creator God, in the beginning you put life into the emptiness, light into the darkness, and saw that it was good. We are created in your image

All: To see good in the light

Leader: You created earth and sky, land and sea, and saw that creation was good. We are created in your image

All: To see good in creation

Leader: You created plants and trees, fruit and flowers in all their colours, and saw that they were good. We are created in your image

All: To see good all around us

Leader: You made the stars and the planets, the sun and the moon in heaven above, and saw that they were good. We are created in your image

All: To see good in heaven above

Leader: Then you created birds that fly in the sky, creatures that swim in the sea, and all kinds of animals that live on the land, and saw that they were good. We are created in your image

All: To see good in the world

Leader: So you created people to live on the earth, to love and be loved, to care for this creation and be fruitful and increase. And you saw it was good, very good. We are created in your image

All: To see good in each other

Leader: And when we failed to praise you for harvests of plenty, to obey your commands and seek your Kingdom and care for the world that you put in our hands, you sent us your Son to show us the way. We are created in his image

All: To see good in the dark

Leader: So look at each other: we are made in God's image, to love and be loved, and find peace from that love.

All: Thank you, Creator of All, that we can see you are good and find peace with each other. Amen

Sharing of the Peace:

Leader: People who sow in peace raise a harvest of justice.
All: We will sow the seeds of peace in each other's hearts.

Share the peace with each other.

Sharing of Bread and Wine

> The bread is broken, the wine is poured,
> the Host is with us, the Spirit is in us,
> and God watches with pleasure as the guests
> gather at the table to receive the seeds of new life.

So take bread, hold it in prayer and remember the Word that was broken and scattered so that we may live.

The grape was taken from the vine and crushed into wine, so take a grape (*or* take this wine) and remember how Jesus pours out his love for our healing and forgiveness.

The above sentences can either follow immediately after each other if people are coming forward for communion, or there can be a pause for distribution followed by an eating and drinking together.

Final Prayer:

> The harvest is plentiful, but the workers are few, so,
>   strengthened by your bread and wine,
> send us out, Lord, into your fields to reap a harvest for the
>   Kingdom to come.

Send us out, to find fertile soil in hearts and minds for your Word to be sown.
All: Together, we will prepare the way and sow the seeds of love.
Send us out, Lord, to clear the rocks and make way for Christ.

All: Together, we will prepare the way and sow the seeds of hope.

Send us out, Lord, to remove the weeds and let the Spirit freely grow.

All: Together, we will prepare the way and sow the seeds of peace.

Lord, send us out, with eyes open to the many fields ripe for harvest where, when we sow together, we can reap with joy the crop of eternal life.

All: Thank you, Lord, for what we have received so that together we may work for you to bring in the harvest. Amen

Richard Becher

Part Six:

The harvest of the land and sea

'You shall eat the fruits of the
labour of your hands'
Genesis 3:19

'Those who sow in tears will reap with
songs of joy.'
Psalm 126:5

Gather Round the Table

The table is laid with a glory of gifts;
here is wholesome bread and golden butter;
here a dish of varied salads, green and red;
beyond it a basket of delicious fruit, multi-coloured,
pears and apples, oranges and melons, grapes and cherries.
Here are wines, red and white, and jugs of clear water.
This is the table of sharing, an expression of caring,
symbol of hospitality
and a reflection of God's abundant gifts for us.
Gather round the table
and may it be a symbol of our unity
and the open hand of compassion.

John Johansen-Berg

Growing Food for Survival: Ethiopia

Kelem Belete lives with his children and grandchildren in a tiny cluster of houses high on the edge of the Ethiopian Rift Valley. The district was badly affected by drought in the 1980s and by civil war in the 1990s. Many of the trees were cut down for firewood and the soil is badly eroded. In the early 2000s these problems have not gone away. They do not disappear.

This family was typical of many in Ethiopia who barely survive on what they grow because the soil is too poor to produce much harvest. Illness or crop disease can push a family into starvation. During times of drought they can't grow their own food so they have to sell their few precious cattle in order to buy something to eat. When it does rain, they have no cattle for ploughing so they are still unable to grow food.

The Ethiopian Orthodox Church supported by Christian Aid has been working with four thousand households to help them improve the soil and grow the food they need to survive. Kelem now grows tomatoes, lettuce, cabbage, beetroot, chilli peppers and apples.

'My family has seen nothing like this before . . . now we can have vegetables whenever we feel like it and we're much healthier now.'

Christian Aid

Fruits of Survival

Instead of dams and dykes, Bangladeshis have revived a traditional practice to survive the biannual monsoons.

When the flood waters in Bangladesh began to rise Fooi Banu realized that this was no ordinary monsoon. The floods threatened to engulf her thatched home and small farm on which she and her two sons depended. A widow for ten years, Banu, aged thirty-three, carved out a living by farming chickens and goats in Sahturia, Manikgarj. But the severe flooding threatened to sweep away the home and farm that had made Banu self-sufficient in the ten years since her husband had died.

Like many Bangladeshis in rural areas, Banu and her sons were reluctant to leave their home and move to higher ground. So they raised their beds above the flood waters, moving on to the roof as the waters lapped higher. Marooned there, with limited food and water, Banu and her sons would not have survived the devastating flooding that lasted more than six weeks in Sahturia. Not, that is, without the help of bananas planted around their home.

Bananas are not just good to eat. Every part of the plant is used in a variety of practical ways. Planted around backyards, the trunks help stabilize the soil. The floppy leaves provide fodder for livestock, can be chopped into plates for food and are also used as umbrellas.

During the monsoon, banana plants are a literal life-saver. By lashing four or five trunks together, rural people can make a raft that is often their only means of transport during floods. This is how Banu and her family survived the floods, fetching water and medicines by raft. 'Without those banana plants, my life would have been much worse than it is now,' says Banu. During the six weeks the flood waters remained high, Banu's sixteen chickens and four goats floated on a raft and ate banana leaves. 'The goats lost weight living on banana leaves for such a long time, but they survived and their health was soon restored after the flood waters subsided,' she said.

Once the flood waters have subsided, villagers use the rich soil washed down by the flood waters to fertilize their land. To stabilize this soil, Banu planted new banana plants. In just over a year, the trees will produce fruit, each plant producing eighty to ninety bananas which she can sell and eat. After harvesting, the stem of the tree is extracted, cooked and served as a vegetable. The rest of the plant is left to rot and fertilize the land.

Typically, each rural family will have between six and ten stands of banana plants around their home. Since the floods of 1998, organizations such as the Christian Commission for Development in Bangladesh, Gono Unnayn Prochestha and Gono Kallayn Trust are encouraging rural people to create small banana plantations around their homes, by offering free training.

For low-paid urban workers, such as rickshaw pullers, factory employees, hawkers, shopkeepers and construction workers, bananas are also a boon, offering a cheap and nutritious lunch. Practical purposes apart, the plant has a symbolic significance for the Hindus. Their elephant-headed god, Ganesh, was married to a banana plant. During the festival of Durga Puza, a banana plant is placed on the altar beside Ganesh, dressed in a sari with ornaments. At a Hindu wedding, the altar is dressed with four banana plants and beneath these the couple are married.

Mohammad Aslam
Bangladesh

New Rice Fields and Fish Ponds

Forty-five families – about 450 people – near Mopti, Mali have received support from the Research Group on Appropriate Technology (GRAT), which is supported by Christian Aid, to help them prepare new rice fields and fish ponds in order to increase rice production and fish stocks. The work was so successful that the project has been expanded and now covers five villages and twenty-three fishing groups in the region.

The villagers depend on the flooding of the nearby Koli-Koli river, which is a tributary of the Niger river, to provide water for growing rice on the river banks. But the floods only come once a year and are unpredictable. GRAT helped them create new paddy fields by building dykes and flooding them by pumping water from the river. This has brought two rice harvests a year. Beside the paddy field another enclosure was built and stocked with tilapia fish to replace the diminishing stocks in the river.

The work was done mainly by local women and children who were delighted with the results. They produced twice as much rice per hectare as before. In the past, most of the women from the area would leave after the harvest to find food elsewhere but now all the women in the group stay. The men work in the millet fields.

The villagers have many problems. The trees have been cut down for building or burning so that women have to walk several miles to find firewood. They have no means of making money to buy food to supplement what they grow; they have no access to clean drinking water and most of the people are illiterate. Christian Aid has responded to these problems with a programme including afforestation, savings and credit schemes, well-digging and literacy classes.

Christian Aid

Eight Bowls of Dough

In Saboba Village in Ghana two women's groups bake and sell bread once a week, working with eight bowls of dough. The product, which is made with wheat flour bought in bulk, sells for 28,000 cedis (£10).

Four women pound the dough together and bake it in an outdoor oven overnight. They sell the bread themselves in Saboba market. The profits are put together for buying grain to store for the dry season.

Christian Aid

Empowering Women

Asmahan Yusuf is a mother of six children and the leader of Yabrud's women's group which is supported by the Palestinian Agricultural Relief Committees (PARC). Normally, she would be involved in everyday activities such as cultivating her almond trees, making jam for selling, or health education. But most Palestinians in the West Bank and Gaza Strip are struggling to live normal lives these days and so Asmahan's role has changed. With piped water supplies regularly running dry, women's groups like Asmahan's are supplying water tanks to their villages in the West Bank.

'We try to empower women at all levels. The women take responsibility for registering people, arranging assessments, and then signing for the tanks,' says programme officer Siham al-Abbasi, who is currently dealing with PARC's emergency work.

The programme is proving effective in helping the women's groups become stronger. 'Now we're stronger as people, and we have better relationships between ourselves,' says group member Im Rabi'a, from nearby Beit Anaan. And she's clear about the support that PARC's women's group can provide in the future: 'We want loans, micro-credit that will help us contribute to our household costs. We don't want handouts. We have to solve our own problems.'

Commitment for Life

201

Farming Together

In Nakpali Village in Ghana the men have realized that it is more productive to farm together rather than alone. They not only help each other on their family farms but also farm together as a group on a 'group plot'. On this plot all expenses and profits are pooled. This group is a member of Konkomba Literacy and Development Programme (KOLADEP) which has provided them with a loan to purchase – in instalments – a pair of bullocks and a plough. The cost is 180,000 cedis (£60).

These farmers' land now produces twice as much as when they cultivated with hand hoes. This group produces enough grain to last the season and is able to sell some surplus for other families to store for the 'hungry season', during March to October.

Christian Aid

Back-breaking Work

It takes Alfonsina and her mother Friada six weeks to harvest their rice crop in Elalane, central Mozambique. Their field isn't large – only one and a half acres – but each swathe of rice has to be cut by hand, using the sharpened edge of a snail shell as a cutting tool. During the season, the women are at work by 5.00 am and they don't leave the fields until it is nearly dark at 5.00 pm. The work is backbreaking but it doesn't end there. Now there is the matter of getting the crop to market. The roads are terrible and there's no transport. In the past, Friada and her daughters had to carry the rice in sacks weighing almost eight stone on their heads to the nearest market, fifteen miles away. This could take up to five hours. So when they arrived they would sell the rice at whatever price it would fetch rather than carry it back again.

All their hard work could end up counting for very little.

Now things are very different. Alfonsina and Friada have joined a local association of women farmers. The association has received a loan from the Rural Association for Mutual

Support (ORAM) which is supported by Christian Aid. This money has helped the women make their hard work go further. They have built a warehouse in Elalane to store the rice until the time when prices are highest. Then the farmers' association hires a tractor to take the crop to market. With the extra profits, the women are hoping to buy a de-husking machine. Rice that has been husked can sell for five times the price.

Christian Aid

Where Apples are Exotic Fruit

Apples are for many people an everyday fruit, taken for granted. They are a common sight in our supermarkets and gardens. But for Worknesh in Ethiopia apples are a special blessing, providing essential vitamins and minerals to supplement her diet. The roots of the apple trees hold the soil together and prevent it from eroding so she can plant cabbages and other vegetables in their shade. An extra harvest can be sold at market as an important source of income.

Apples have improved life for Worknesh and her family. Here is just one of many families for whom finding enough food to live on is a constant concern.

Christian Aid

Land of Gold

Let us pray
　　　for Bangladesh:

the poet's 'land of gold',
whose fields produce rich harvests,
whose rivers, streams and pukurs* give
a huge catch of fish.

* A pukur is a man-made pond in the middle of a town or village which may be used for fish-farming, as a reservoir for drinking and as washing water for people and animals.

Let us pray
        for people:

who work in temperatures
that would cause us to wilt.
For children
who are survivors of much suffering,
tested more than most of us
will ever experience.

Let us pray:
        that their special riches

may inspire us
to offer what we can from the blessings
you have given us.
Lord, help us to see the world
with your eyes.

John Crocker

By the Sweat of Your Brow You Shall Eat Your Food

For those who sweat
under the hot sun,
working the dry ground,
longing for rain
we pray: God let them see
the fruits of their labours.

For those who sweat
in heavy industries,
sweat running dry
as one by one the furnaces
are switched off
we pray: God let them see
the fruits of their labours.

For those who worry in the night,
sweating over a decision,
whom to make redundant
whether this firm can keep going,
we pray: God let them see
the fruits of their labours.

For those who sweat
in someone else's field,
at someone else's workbench,
fingers raw and tempers frayed,
for peace . . .
we pray: God let them see
the fruits of their labours.

For each of us,
when we have deadlines
rushed jobs,
when we do not know
if we, or our work,
are accepted or rejected,
when we sweat over it,
we pray: God let us see
the fruits of our labours.

Bob Warwicker

An Industrial Harvest

Creating God
who fashioned the universe
hung stars in space in the precision
of chaos,
crafted the earth
planted a garden,
made humankind from dust
able to bear your image,
share your work,

we confess our failure
to provide good work for all,
our greed for profit
which creates pressures on working people
to produce more for less,
our indifference to the working conditions of others
which allows poor safety regulations,
machinery not properly maintained, inadequate resources,
workers too tired to concentrate
so that accidents become all too possible.

Loving God
we pray for all working people.
Give them strength and courage
and satisfaction in the work they do.

We pray for
those whose decisions have direct effects
on pay and conditions and security of work
– managers and directors and politicians.
Give them clarity about the results
of their decisions on the lives of others
and courage and wisdom to make right judgements.

Forgiving God
we pray for ourselves
in the work we do every day.
Give us diligence and enthusiasm and insight
to affirm good working practice,
courage and persistence
to point to injustice and right wrong,
gentleness to work to reconcile differences.

Help us all to work for a just community
in which work and rest and worship are properly valued

so that everyone can share in your work of creation
with joy.
In the name of Jesus Christ
Amen.

Heather Pencavel

The Agricultural Blacksmith

Brindawathi, her husband, Drimba Kadraka, their son, Sad-
haram, and their daughter, Hemawathi, belong to the Kond
tribe, one of the sixty-seven tribes of Orissa in north-east India.
They each play their part in the production of agricultural
tools which they sell to people in surrounding villages.

They live in a very remote village in a hilly part of the
district of Rayagada. The area around them has many rice
paddies and at harvest time it is very colourful when the
mustard crop is in full bloom.

However, behind this rural façade there is no proper sanitation, no access to safe water and no electricity. It is not easily
accessible by road and the community fears the influence of
mainstream society. The nearest main road is five kilometres
away and it is a long uphill walk. In recent times many of the
Adivasi people died of starvation after being forced off their
land and with no access to the forest they lost their source of
livelihood.

PREPARE, a Christian Aid-funded organization, has been
working in Orissa state with tribal people – the Adivasi – for
more than ten years. Funding has been directed towards
people such as Brindawathi and Drimba to help them earn a
living. As they were already skilled blacksmiths facilities were
provided to help them keep alive the traditional tribal skill.
They were able to buy a new blower and purchase scrap iron.
Until recently they were using the traditional methods for
firing their agricultural tools. This meant hours of pumping by
pedalling a simple foot mechanism which proved to be both
labour-intensive and inefficient. Brindawathi says, 'The new

equipment has helped us to produce more tools with greater speed and has also increased our income.' When using the traditional method they were able only to supply one village with tools but now they can supply tools for four villages.

Through the intervention of PREPARE and the consent of the Adivasi people, a federation of blacksmiths was formed bringing together the blacksmiths from five villages. Women like Brindawathi are looking to become members of the Blacksmiths' Committee. Drimba is very supportive of his wife who has now been working as a blacksmith for several years. 'My husband encourages me. It will take some time for the others to agree to women members but I am confident that it will happen,' says Brindawathi.

Christian Aid

A Litany of the Ocean

The horizon is so far away;
the waves surge for ever
and the ocean currents travel the globe.

**Our boat is so small
God's ocean is great**.

When the breakers shake the rocks,
and the storm crests splinter in foam;
when the salt spray stings the eyes
and the gulls flee inland

**Our boat is so small
and God's ocean so strong**.

Then the sea glistens and glows in the sun
with colours like a song;
shallows and deeps
and restless tides sing noon and vespers.

Our boat is so small
        and God's ocean so alive.

The wealth of the sea is its life,
to restore the balance of nature,
to abound in the first living things
and the species that feed us all.

        Our boat is so small
        and God's provision so great.

Our harvesting can become plunder
as we drive species towards extinction,
not out of wickedness, but
for food, for profit, for human need.

        Our nets are so urgent
        and God's gifts so long in the making.

In the great ocean of God's eternal purpose
we often seem small
and our life so short
and our understanding so childish.
But our human needs are so great
and rapidly expanding
that we upset the balance of boat and sea.

        Holy Spirit, mover of the waters,
        teach us God's goodness
        and the glory of creation,
        so that we may sail with confidence
        and with humility through the ages of life.

Bernard Thorogood
Australia

Fish Become Big Business

Mary Aheto and fellow members of the women's fish smoking groups share a strong sense of achievement. Despite high inflation, their savings have grown. They are building a school and latrines for their villages, five fishing villages some thirty-seven miles from Accra, the capital of Ghana. Some, like Mary, a founder of the Chokomey Village group, have built houses for themselves. Their self-confidence is on the march. 'Our men are proud of their business women,' said one of the group.

The secret of their success is the training they get in business management skills, the development of more efficient fish smoking and storage techniques and the strength of the groups they have formed to manage loans.

The women buy fish direct from the boats and smoke them to preserve them. They then sell them through inland markets. They laugh at the days when they were cheated by dealers who, in buying fish by the basket, presented bigger baskets to be filled. They soon got wise to these tricks.

When they were asked what they value most about their project, the women answered variously:

'Now our village has proper latrines';

'We can buy clothes and build houses for ourselves.'

In all of this they have been supported by Christian Aid's partner the Freedom from Hunger Campaign (FFHC). Recently the project received £39,000 from Christian Aid and £21,000 from Comic Relief.

Mary Aheto, who now owns six fish smoking ovens, is particularly proud that all her children are being educated.

Christian Aid

Harvest of the Sea

Various children and adults will be needed for this roleplay, also suitable props for the action.

Narrator   Jesus chose fishermen to be his first disciples. One day Simon and Andrew were fishing with nets beside Lake Galilee, when Jesus came along.

(Simon and Andrew mime fishing)

Jesus   Come with me and I will teach you to catch people.

Narrator   Simon and Andrew left their nets and went with Jesus. A bit further on, James and John were with their father, Zebedee, in their boat, getting their nets ready to go fishing.

Jesus   Come with me and I will teach you to catch people.

Narrator   James and John left their father in the boat and went with Jesus and Simon and Andrew.

Prayer:

Narrator   Today a lot of people have jobs that take them out to sea. Sometimes it can be very dangerous.

Fisherman   I'm a fisherman and I still go out in my boat and catch fish in my net so that people can enjoy tasty, healthy fish.

Narrator   We pray for all fishermen out at sea. Please keep them safe in stormy weather.

211

Roughneck	I work on an oil rig, drilling for oil that is used for fuel and in industry.
Narrator	We pray for all who work on the oil rigs. Please keep them safe and be with their families who have to spend many weeks without them.
Ferry Staff	I look after you on the ferry when you travel on it as a part of your holiday.
Narrator	We pray for all the crew of ferries. Give them patience and understanding and help them always to check that equipment is safe.
Lifeboat Person	I go out in the lifeboat and rescue people who get into difficulties with their boats.
Narrator	We pray for all those who go out in lifeboats. Give them courage and strength as they face danger. Be with their families who wait at home.
Mission Organization Person	When there is an accident at sea I visit the families and wait with them for news. If it is good news I can be happy with them but if it is bad news then I try to help them in every way that I can.
Narrator	We pray for all who work for the Mission Organizations for those at sea. Please show them how they can be of help to people when they most need it. Help them to show your love to others as they do this special work.
All	**Amen**

Heather Johnston

Blessing the Boats

This liturgy of Blessing the Boats has been revived by a rural community in north Northumberland, UK. The 'bread' in the prayers is fish-shaped biscuits which are either shared or, if the tide is in, cast on the waters.

Holy God,
as you called Noah
to make a boat to rescue your people.
as you parted the Red Sea to let your people pass,
as you rescued Jonah from the belly of the big fish,
as you walked on water and stilled the storm,
as you called fisherfolk from their nets
to fish for people,

> Rescue us,
> deliver us from our slavery,
> still our fear,
> calm our minds,
> call us to pilgrimage.

Bless those who guard our coast,
those who watch over the waters.
Bless those who wrench a living from the sea
and those who harvest the produce of the deep.

Bless those who offer hospitality
and those who are received as guests.
Bless those who come as sightseers
and continue as pilgrims.

Bless us and this community
and as we cast our bread
on the waters of your creation
renew us in faith and unity.

or

Bless us and this community
and as we share bread together
renew us in faith and unity.

Kate McIlhagga

Fingerling Cultivation

Rabea Begum's house in Jatpur, Bangladesh, is next to a large ditch that was dug out to raise the house site above the level of the surrounding flooded rice fields. The pond that developed has provided water and a washing place for the whole family since then but it was Rabea who first thought of using the pond as a nursery for breeding and growing fish. Unfortunately, Rabea's first attempts at nursery fish farming were unsuccessful. She had paid too much for fish spawn and did not sell the fingerlings before the dry season when many of them died in the shrinking pool and increasingly stagnant water.

She did not give up but learned from her first attempt. The second time she was more careful about the carp spawn she bought with advice and credit from Intermediate Technology and the local partner, Shurja Mukhi Women's Group. After rearing the spawn for seventy days she sold her fish quickly and made a profit. From these profits she was able to loan money to her husband for rice trading and still have enough left over to buy herself a new sari. Now that Rabea has confidence in her abilities she wants to continue producing fingerlings without credit support.

Intermediate Technology
Bangladesh

A prayer to accompany the above story:

God of Resourcefulness

Creator God,
Giver of Life
in a variety of ways,
Thank you for the resourcefulness of women and men
in developing countries.

Creator God,
Giver of Life
whereby harvests are sustained,
Thank you for the resilience of women and men
who persevere in their local communities.

Creator God,
Giver of Life,
giving benefits to families,
Thank you for the ways in which people work together
for the common good.

We give you humble thanks,
We give you heartfelt praise,
Amen

Geoffrey Duncan

On Practical Sharing

In the late 1980s my family and I lived in the poor urban area of Dumaguete, a small city in the central part of the Philippine Islands. I was working with a programme to empower people of the depressed slum areas by helping them realize their rights and raising their consciousness about the roots of the poverty they were experiencing.

My own family's income could hardly make ends meet even if we tried hard to live a simple lifestyle. My neighbours earned their living mostly as laundry-women, motorcab drivers, labourers and vendors. Always, life had been difficult.

Children were malnourished and protein-rich foods were becoming expensive. The people participated in protests against price rises of basic commodities, militarization and the suppression of the basic rights of workers in the local areas.

I took my children even when they were infants to the protest rallies. I tried to inculcate among the children and parents the connection between a simple lifestyle and sharing, these being basically rooted in the teachings of Jesus Christ. We started a tradition of sharing with our neighbours rice, fish, meat or anything available when our family would receive any unexpected money that I earned from some extra work such as facilitating workshops or writing.

One morning my husband came home from the mountains where he was pastoring a church, bringing two kilos of shelled peanuts. I had been wanting to make home-made peanut butter because I could not afford the very expensive commercial brands sold in the grocery stores. I was excited thinking that my kids, Nabi aged four and Dev aged two, would enjoy cheap and real peanut butter.

As I walked past the small houses of my neighbours that evening, returning from work, I was thinking about making the peanut butter when neighbours greeted me with sweet 'Thank yous'. As I got closer to the house we were renting another neighbour looked out from her window and said, 'Nanay,* thank you!'

Perplexed, I asked, 'What are you thanking me for?'

My neighbour, Joy, answered, 'Oh, Nabi went around distributing peanuts. The peanuts were good.'

Trying to hide my shock, I politely said, 'You're welcome.' But deep within I was troubled. I didn't know if I would be angry or be proud of Nabi. Payday was still two weeks away and there was little money left in my wallet after buying basic foodstuffs. I raced up the wobbly stairs and checked the plastic bag that contained the peanuts. They could have made a one-month supply of vegetable protein for the children, but my

* *Nanay* is a Cebuano word equivalent to Mamma or Mother.

son had given them away – leaving just about two cups for us.

I called Nabi and asked, 'Why did you give away the peanuts? Don't you know that I planned to make peanut butter with them for you?'

The four-year-old, looking happy and proud that he had accomplished something, answered, 'I shared them with our neighbours. I thought we had too much.'

I heard him, but I heard him, hard. I wanted to tell him 'Not this time!' but nothing came out of my mouth. I just looked at my husband and said, 'Well, that is fine. But next time, we should plan together the giving away of peanuts, okay?'

My husband's salary as a rural pastor amounted to about the equivalent of $50 a month. I would say we were certainly at the poverty level according to the official economic index at that time. But most of our neighbours didn't even have fixed wages or a payday to look forward to. They were below the poverty level. They lived one day at a time.

Sometimes, or I should say, most of the time, it is easy for us adults to say or preach about sharing. But to practise it is difficult. If people will only take seriously the principle of simple lifestyle and share and globalize it, instead of globalizing the greed for profit at the expense of many, wouldn't this be a wonderful world to live in? It's a paradox but Jesus is right: we need to become like children . . . for indeed, little children lead us with their simple and innocent wisdom.

Muriel Orevillo-Montenegro
The Philippines

Farmers' Festival

This is a time to give thanks
for the talents and work of farmers;
for the variety of crops they produce;
for their faithfulness through times of hardship;
for their loving care of domestic animals;
for their patience in the tasks through changing seasons;

for their shared hopes for the future.
Now is a time to share in the festival
and join the farmers' celebration of the harvest.

John Johansen-Berg

Be Careful with the Earth's Gifts

Leader: At this time of year the leaves on trees start to change colour: yellows, reds and oranges. Soon they will fall to the ground and the colours will fade. But the leaves are not wasted. They will rot and go back into the earth, feeding the soil with goodness for new plants to grow. In this way life's circle begins again.

Harvest is a time for being grateful – for food and water, for air, warmth and light. And as we say thank you, we can also promise to be careful with the earth's gifts.

Earth's Gifts

Leader: In the beginning the earth was made, round and blue and beautiful.

(A child brings a globe to the front of the church and places it on a table)

Earth was spinning, bright and new and beautiful in space.

In the beginning earth was full of gifts: oceans and seas
splashing,
crashing.
Valleys and mountains
dipping,
soaring.

218

Animals and plants
creeping,
springing.
And all the peoples of
the earth
living and talking
together.
The earth and
everything in it
was beautiful.

*(Two children bring a brown cloth to the front of
the church and lay it across a table, saying:)*

We bring brown,
colour of earth,
source of growth,
surrounding and feeding
sleeping seeds.

*(Two children bring a blue cloth to the front of the
church and lay it across a table, saying:)*

We bring blue,
colour of water,
source of life,
refreshing and cleansing
people and land.

*(Two children bring a white cloth to the front of the
church and lay it across a table, saying:)*

We bring white,
colour of air,
source of breath,
moving and shaking
sky and trees.

(Two children bring a red cloth to the front of the church and lay it across a table, saying:)

> We bring red,
> colour of fire,
> source of energy,
> warming and giving life
> to growing things.

All: **We say thank you
for life and for the gifts
of the earth**.

Around the Earth

Leader: The earth is used carefully by some of the people who live in Andra Pradesh, a state in south India, and in Malawi, a country in Africa.

Many people who live in these places depend on the land for their living. They know that worms and left-over husks of corn can help grow enough food for people and their families.

Reader One: It is very dry in Andra Pradesh so growing crops is difficult. Christian Aid has helped to set up Pacha Saale – The Green School – where students learn about farming. Kavita is a student there.

Interviewer: Hello, Kavita.

Kavita: Hello.

Interviewer: I've never heard of a green school before. What is it?

Kavita: It's what you call 'eco-friendly'. We learn subjects such as English and Maths. But we also learn about the land and how to take care of it.

Interviewer: How does your school help you to farm?

Kavita: We learn how to farm without damaging the earth. We don't use expensive chemicals – instead we learn how to turn waste, like manure, into useful fertilizers for the soil. We learn about worms and how they are good for the soil.

Reader Two: Elizabeth Hara is from Ekwendi in Malawi, southern Africa. The only money Elizabeth earns is from selling corn that she grows in a small field.

Reader Three: Each morning, Elizabeth goes to her field at about 4.00 am and works until 8.00 am. Then it becomes too hot so she goes home, feeds her grandchildren, fetches water and looks after her husband.

Elizabeth: The children were often crying for food. Now we have enough to eat.

Reader: Christian Aid has helped to pay for a project which helps people in Malawi grow food for their families. Elizabeth learned how to re-use corn husks to make compost for the soil. This makes the soil better for growing crops.

Prayer:

Thank you God
for this earth–
for us to enjoy,
for us to live in,
for us to
take care of.

At this harvest time
we bring our thanks
for all the earth's gifts.
We make our promises
to share what we have
and to care for our world.
Amen

Christian Aid

Starvation within Harvest

Starvation within Harvest!

Have you ever noticed that the English word 'harvest' can be altered to a word that means the very opposite? It can be altered to an anagram meaning the total lack of necessary resources for life. Set aside the 'h' of harvest to make 'arvest', bring the last two letters to the fore, and there is 'starve'. It is ironic that within the noun meaning 'gathered-in supplies' is a verb meaning the total lack of the same.

And what might the 'h' stand for – Hope, Health, Happiness, Hell, Hopelessness?
Harvest implies Health.
Harvest implies Happy Completion of sowing and reaping.
'H' is also for Helpless.
Humankind feels helpless about the starvation of millions of people. The starving people feel helpless.

How do we ensure that the 'h' factor of harvest allows for
distribution of supplies?
In humility we pray:

O God of Harvest, great and various,
help us to find ways, large, little and diverse,
to co-operate with creation;
to re-structure our economies;
to share our harvests
so that the potential to 'starve' hidden within 'harvest' is not
activated
but remains a warning that the good 'harvest' may not last as
such;
that harvest should be hope for all, therefore healthy harvests
need to continue.
May we always value fruitfulness from planting as a gift from
You, Creator God,
and use it wisely and generously.
Amen.

Glenn Jetta Barclay
Aotearoa New Zealand/Northern Ireland

The Complexity of Global Forces

God of all power and might,
you are far beyond our capacity to understand,
but you have made yourself known to us
in the person of Jesus;
give encouragement and insight
to all whose labours are caught up in the
complexity of global forces,
that they may not feel overwhelmed,
but know for themselves the value of their efforts.

Christopher P. Burkett

For the Pressure of Work

Jesus, who called your disciples aside
to rest awhile,
hear our prayer for all workers
bowed down by their labours:
to the tired, bring refreshment,
to the stressed, bring peace of heart,
to the pressured, bring rest,
to the exploited, bring a just reward,
and all for your mercy's sake,
you who laboured for the health of our souls.

Christopher P. Burkett

Behind and Within

Eucharist is the feast of seeing behind and within,
behind the bread to the sales assistant,
baker, miller, farmer; to the plant, the seed,
the earth, to the sun and moon, air and water;
to the cosmic explosion that birthed universe,
to the God who is in all
and through all.
And also the knowledge that our eating starts another
process that leads back to the earth and
the perpetual recycling of the atoms,
temporarily part and parcel of this bread,
this particular part of the body of Christ.
Indeed the divine that is in this bread is sign and symbol
of the sacred process of recycling.

William L. Wallace
Aotearoa New Zealand

A Response to God's Generosity

It all begins with God
Creator, Sustainer, Provider
Who loves and shares and gives
Who covenants and cares
Abundantly
God

We respond
As we see God
Big God
Small God
Big Creator
Small Creator
Big Provider
Small Provider

It all begins with God

The Harvest Festival has always been special to me. This is primarily because of my home congregation and how I experienced the festival from my earliest days. You see, for many of those people, God was awesome. Consequently, when Harvest Festival came around they were excited to bring gifts to this awesome God who had redeemed them in Jesus Christ. They brought the best of the crops they had grown.

Some planted regularly, some planted specially for Harvest. If the yield did not come in time for Harvest they were disappointed. Those who did not plant bought things from the market to place on the harvest table or they gave a very special offering. There was produce from animals. Some persons made delicacies for the harvest table. People gave a special offering at Harvest even if they had brought other gifts. This was a special time of praise because God had been faithful to them throughout the year. Even the clothes were special and the singing!

The church building was well decorated with coconut, palm and bamboo branches. The excitement began with the preparation on Saturday afternoon – rehearsing, decorating, bringing gifts. God had been GOOD. Persons had looked to God to care for them and bring them through and God had done it. Even in their times of testing they had been able to see the hand of God and experience God's joy. God had been generous. It was their time to give generously to an awesome God.

The example of the people from my home congregation taught me about giving as a response to God's generosity. Also, it taught me that when people value God and recognize God's goodness and mercy they give a lot, even when they do not have a lot to give.

Prayer:

> Generous Creator, Sustainer
> Loving, Caring, Sharing God
> **We give you praise**
>
> For your Providence and mercy
> For your redeeming grace
> **We give you praise**
>
> You are God
> Beyond our comprehension
> Simply Awesome in all you do and are
> **We give you praise**
>
> For the times of testing
> For the times when we wondered where you were
> For the times when you upheld us
> **We give you praise**
>
> We confess the times when we fail to recognize you
> The times when we seek to limit you
> The times when we do not acknowledge you
> **Lord, forgive us**

We confess that we take you for granted
We do not see you in the harvest
We do not see you in our work
We do not see you in our productivity
Lord, forgive us

Because we do not see you
Because we limit you
We fail you
Lord, forgive us

We fail you in our relationships with each other, with
creation, with yourself
In our stewardship of time, money, creation, the Gospel
In our response to all that you are and all that you do
Lord, forgive us

We ask for a new vision of yourself
A new heart for you
A new heart for each other
A new heart for your created order
Lord, empower us

Teach us anew who you are
That we may respond to you in generosity
In caring for each other
In caring for your world
In caring for you
Lord, empower us

May harvest be a sign for us
Not only that you covenant with us
But that we covenant with you
To be good, generous and faithful stewards of all that you
entrust to us
Lord, empower us

Lord, we acknowledge you as the one who created every-thing, who upholds everything, who provides for us. Give us the grace and strength to give ourselves and all that we have to you. **Amen**

Claire Smith
Guyana

A Day in the Life of a Breadmaker

My husband and I get up at five in the morning. He makes his way to the fields. I collect the flour, salt, yeast, kindling wood and water that I need for the bakery. This takes several jour-neys with heavy loads even though it is only a few minutes' walk. I pay the foreman in advance and leave the bakers to transform my ingredients into dough. I set to work making peanut butter – enough to last several weeks – but often before this is finished I need to leave the house for the bakery as the dough will be ready and I must shape it into small loaves. Then it needs to be put in the ovens. Then I return home to fin-ish my cooking. There are other chores – cleaning the house, washing the clothes, feeding the chickens.

Then it is off to the bakery once more taking my large wicker basket to collect the bread. The smell of freshly baked bread is wonderfully appetizing but I've no time to eat right now. Better that I take it into town to sell from my stall. I sell the bread on its own or with peanut butter to those who feel able to treat themselves. In a quiet moment I realize how hungry I've become so I eat a little of my stock. It's late evening by the time I get home. There is a lot of bread left over so I'll be able to sell all day tomorrow. My husband has pre-pared a simple meal for the family. He is a good man.

I used to borrow from the loan sharks, paying back much more than I had borrowed. I didn't believe that I was capable of running a small business. Then the Church set up a com-munity bank for women like me: we call it the *gwoupman* which means 'club'. The gwoupman has taught us how to plan financially, how to calculate profits and costs. Also, it gave us loans at low interest rates. Now I can buy ingredients in bulk and pay back my loan. We work hard as we're eager to make this scheme a success. If the programme moves on to the next town, we'll carry on with the *gwoupman* ourselves – helping each other and helping ourselves. In time I hope to be able to save enough to build my own large oven so that I don't have to use the bakery. That's my ambition.

Christian Aid

God, Maker and Breaker of Bread

Breadmaking God,
providing food for your children
with an abundance that surpasses our hopes,
we praise you.

**God, Maker and Breaker of Bread,
feed and nourish us with your love.**

Breadmaking God,
working with those who sweat and struggle
to provide food and nourishment for the hungry,
bring justice to your world.

**God, Maker and Breaker of Bread,
feed and nourish us with your love.**

Breadmaking God,
hearing our greedy clamour for more,
our desire for possessions surplus to our needs,
forgive us.

**God, Maker and Breaker of Bread,
feed and nourish us with your love.**

Breadmaking God,
offering us the bread of life,
mysterious in its brokenness,
feed us.

**God, Maker and Breaker of Bread,
feed and nourish us with your love**.

Jan Berry

Major Indian Field Crops

An awakening and an awareness of how we need each other in our global situation – a time of chapattis, roti, sesame seed rolls, chutneys, basmati rice, sunflower oil . . . We enjoy our breakfasts, we cook or dine out. Our harvests are interdependent.

Cereals, pulses and oil seeds provide a diverse harvest – except when crops fail due to lack of rain, causing drought, or conversely cannot be harvested because of too much rain and consequent flooding!

Cereals

Rice

Rice is the staple food of humid areas in south India. It's grown in about 25 per cent of the agricultural land in India. It prefers low-lying and water-logged areas where none of the other cereals can be grown.

Wheat

Amongst cereals wheat is the second most cultivated crop in India, rice being the first. In India wheat is popularly consumed by human beings in the form of chapattis, purees, parathas and upama, and as wheat straw by livestock.

Sorghum

Sorghum is known for its drought tolerance and is the most popular food and fodder crop of dry areas of India. Sorghum grain is used as human food in the form of chapattis. It is also cooked like rice, malted, fed to cattle and used as poultry feed. Its green fodder is used as important fodder throughout the country.

Bajra

Bajra is grown for grain as well as forage purposes in about 12 million hectares and produces grain worth about 11 per cent of the total cereal production. It is a popular crop in the areas where sorghum is grown except that it is more resistant to moisture stress conditions. Bajra grain is used as human food in the form of rotis or chapattis. Its green fodder and dried stover are used as important fodder for livestock.

Pulses

Green Gram

The crop is grown mostly during the rain-fed Kharif season (June–September). It's used mainly as dal preparation and as sprouted grains to mix with salads.

Pigeon Pea (Red Gram)

It is the most important dal (pulse) of entire India. The crop cannot withstand waterlogging at any stage of growth. Frost is fatal to the crop but because of its deeper root system it can withstand severe drought. It needs bright sunny days during flowering and a dry period during the maturity of its pods. It's used as a dal every day either with rice or chapattis, and has a very high protein content.

Oil Seeds

Groundnut

Groundnut is the most important oil seed crop grown in India. It prefers sandy to sandy-loam soils having good drainage facilities, as heavy soils are not suitable for the groundnut crop.

Groundnut oil is edible oil. It finds extensive use as a cooking medium both as refined oil and vanaspati ghee. It is also used in soap making, and manufacturing cosmetics and lubricants. It is an important protein supplement in cattle and poultry rations. It is also consumed as a confectionery product. Groundnut shells are used as fuel for preparing rotis, chapattis and so on. Many people also prepare a groundnut chutney with salt and dry chilli powder. This they use with rotis and curd (yoghurt) for breakfast in the rural areas.

Sesame

Sesamum, also known as sesame, til and gingerly, is an important and ancient oil-yielding crop.

The sesame seed is a rich source of edible oil. Sesame oil is used as a cooking oil in southern India. It is also used for anointing the body, for manufacturing perfumed oils and for medicinal purposes. Sesame-cake is a rich source of protein, carbohydrates and mineral nutrients, such as calcium and phosphorus. It is also a valuable and nutritious feed for milk cattle.

Sunflower

The sunflower is mainly grown for its oil. The oil is used for culinary purposes, in the preparation of vanaspati and in the manufacture of soaps and cosmetics. It is especially recommended for heart patients. Its cake is rich in protein and is used as a cattle and poultry feed.

Anil Kumar Patil
South India

A Prayer for the Harvests of Cereals, Pulses and Oils

Lord of the Diverse Harvests,
 focus our minds on the importance of
  cereals
   pulses
    oil seeds
 and the daily diet of women and men
 around our globe,
  in their local communities, villages, towns, cities.

Thank you, Lord of the Diverse Harvests
 for the loving care of the farmers
 as they sow the seeds;
 as they nurture the crops,
 for their resilience and resourcefulness
 as they meet and overcome difficulties.

Forgive us, Lord of the Diverse Harvests
 for the many occasions
 when we ignore or forget the importance of staple
  diets,
 of basic foods which are necessary
 for people, especially children.
 (We indulge in our multi-vitamin-supplemented
 over-conscious well-person diets.)

Encourage us, Lord of the Diverse Harvest
 to search our local markets,
 our supermarket shelves for Fair Trade products,
 our organic suppliers,
 our Indian stores in our multi-cultural communities
 so that we can share in the rich tastes of their culture.

Lord of the Diverse Harvests
 motivate men and women
 with knowledge and wisdom

– the sheer desire to help –
to take time out to pool their expertise
with the cultural knowledge of the farmers.
Enable them to know that they are needed,
that precious lives depend on partnerships
of shared experiences.

Lord of the Diverse Harvests
> lead us
> in the direction of working creatively
> with skilled minds
> in our love for people:
> to go and not to count the cost.

Geoffrey Duncan

God of Rice and Chapatti

1 Timothy 6:17–19; Isaiah 55:1–3a

God of corn and bread, of rice and chapatti,
we thank you for our food
and for the immense variety available to us.
We thank you for research that enables food
to be grown
without destruction of the earth,
for developments that improve storage
so we waste less.
We pray for all who live and work
in rural communities,
for all who work the land
in this country and all over the world.
We pray for a more equal sharing
of the resources of the earth.
> Lord, in your mercy
> **Hear our prayer**.

Jenny Spouge

Paddy Fields

Hooved feet
tramp the dust
in an endless march;
shoulders drag
a heavy wooden plough
turning over clods of rich soil.

Then the fields are flooded;
hard steps
become shining miniature lakes,
layered mud-beds.

Finally
with skirts held up
tucked in tight belts,
backs bent
feet bare
legs wading through wet slime;
busy hands
tenderly root
green rice-plants
deep into the murky soil;

colouring in the valley
with the lush green promise of harvest.

Alison Leishman
England/Bhutan

Thank Him

Thank him for bread that's daily given.
Thank him for lilies dressed in gold;
Thank him for birds and beasts unanxious
In the Shepherd's fold.

Thank him for fishermen and fishing,
Thank him for towns of Galilee;
Thank him for friends and homes enfolding
Peace like Bethany.

Thank him for fields that sparkle morning,
Thank him for breakfast on the shore;
Thank him for hills that speak in sunrise,
Life for evermore.

Tune: Danke
and for variation each verse can be pitched higher by a semitone

Norwyn Denny

Harvest Eucharist

Note that all parts of this Eucharist in bold type are intended to be spoken by the whole congregation.

Opening Sentence:

Here, now, you are invited to leave your deserts and toil.
Here, now, Jesus beckons.
Come to the feast that has grown from the love of God.
Listen to his voice.
In him your harvest has been gathered.
Come.

For in him all the fullness of God was pleased to dwell, and through him God was pleased to reconcile to himself all things, whether on earth or in heaven, by making peace through the blood of his cross (Colossians 1: 19–20).

Collect:

God of life, death, and astonishing new life,
you sing your resurrection into each new sunrise,
each pregnant moment,
every new-born hope.
Teach us now your song
that we may open our barren hearts to your words
and hear your promise of harvest.

Suggested Readings:

Old Testament: Deuteronomy 8:1–18; 22:1–4; Genesis 1 : 24–31; Psalm 104; Micah 4:1–5.
New Testament: Romans 8:18–25; 1 Corinthians 3:1–9; 2 Corinthians 9:6–15; Galatians 6:1–10; Philippians 2:1–13.
Gospel: Matthew 6:19–34; 9:35–38; Mark 4:26–34; Luke 9:12–17; John 4:31–38; 6:41–59.

Prayers:

These prayers are in four sections. Use four readers – children if possible. For visual impact, arrange for children to provide suitably decorated notices to hold as the prayers are read.

Ploughing

As the land is torn open for sowing,
so plough apart our stubborn hearts.
Pull out the weeds with wild love.
Let the heat and ice of your holiness
cleanse our soil.
Open our eyes to the need around us,
and prepare us for you.
This, by your Spirit, we pray for.

Sowing

For the heart to feel the pain of the farmer
whose stock has been lost;
for compassion on communities caught
in a spiral of hopelessness and despair;
for the will to proclaim we pay *more* for our produce
in order to give our fair share;
for a harvest that offers the love of our Lord
in our thanks for the food we have here.
These are the seeds we pray for.

Growing

As stewards of creation, called to care,
we see the abuse and over-use
demanded by our disposable lifestyle.
We weep in our own dust, and wish for better.
May we grow in your grace and take our place
to admit our fault. May our spirits revolt
against our smiling selfishness
and be willing to call, weep, work for a Harvest
of hope for all.
This is the hope we strive for.

Reaping

It is our decisions that hurt and harm.
Often it is others who reap the consequences
of all that we sow badly.
So, for those of us who handle Harvest
only through the supermarket shelves,
may we consider what our buying power may do.
And may we all reap a rich Harvest of our deeds and words.
This is the Harvest we desire.

The Peace:

Pass around a basket of large (e.g. sunflower) seeds. Ask each person to take a seed and offer it to their neighbour as a sign of life and hope, whilst they share the Peace. You may wish to say:

Every seed must die to grow.
So our Lord was thrust into darkness for the life we may hold.
He is our peace and our hope.
> **Thanks be to God.**

The Bread and Wine – A Responsive:

You may wish to break the bread and share during the first (bread) part of this responsive, then pour the wine and share during the second (wine) part. Alternatively, breaking, pouring and sharing may all be done together at the end of the responsive.

What is this bread?

> **This is the sign of grace, the manna from heaven.**
> **It is the stuff of life itself, our nourishment in the deserts we cross.**

What is it for?

> **This is for our feeding, to keep us walking together.**
> **It is for us, our body and spirit, to bind us to God in love.**

Who is it from?

This is the gift of God, who loves and sustains us.
It is given without holding back, part of God's invitation to us all.

What is this bread?

This is the Body of Christ, he who was tempted to feed
   himself, but, for us, did not.
He is the true Bread of Life, who was broken and scattered,
   like crumbs on the water, in love.
This bread is part of us, our harvest, for ever, in him.
Thanks be to God.

What is this wine?

This is the joy of living, the best of the wedding.
It is the death of the grape, and the cup of Thanksgiving.

What is it for?

This is for slaking our thirst, for binding us together.
It is for completing our meal, and for lifting to God in
   thanks.

Who is it from?

This is the gift of God, who loves and sustains us.
It is given without holding back, part of God's invitation to
   us all.

What is this wine?

This is the Blood of Christ,
he who shared wine with his disciples, and calls us to share
   also.
He is the wine of the Kingdom of God, spilt out in offering;
his blood shed to form a river to God, that we all may wash
   and be cleansed.
This wine is both pain and joy.
Thanks be to God.

Concluding Praise:

We give thanks for food, the life-giver.
We give thanks for land, and the turning of seasons.
We give thanks for those who toil for our convenience.
And we commit ourselves to act thankfully and thoughtfully,
in the products we buy, the amount we pay,
the places we shop.
We commit ourselves to God's Harvest–
the gathering, in love, of all that is good.
We commit ourselves to Jesus, the seed of God,
crushed and broken for this world,
that the Harvest may be glorious.

Blessing:

May you let the Spirit of God tend you.
May the seed of Jesus grow within you, strong and true.
May God the Father bring your fruit to maturity,
And may the love of God multiply,
forty, sixty, one hundred fold,
through all you do.
Amen

Duncan L. Tuck

Part Seven:

Prayers, graces and blessings

'Let us give thanks to the Lord our God.
It is right to give thanks and praise.'

Common Worship

Call to Worship

Let us worship God,
the God who forms the rhythm
of our lives
the God who is present
at the beginning and ending
of each day . . . each season . . .
each purpose.

Kate McIllhagga

Dear God

Thank you for the lovely people
who sing for harvest.
I hope you can come and look through the window
of my school.
Amen.

Louisa Fenn

A Eucharistic Blessing

Lord, when you broke bread with the two disciples at
Emmaus you made scales fall from their eyes and they recog-
nized you. Come to us now and enlighten the eyes of our mind
to the reality of your risen presence and to the needs of others.
Bless us and the bread we are about to break.
Amen.

Pax Christi

Eucharistic Prayer for a Quiet Garden Day

The Lord is here
His spirit is with us

Lift up your hearts,
We lift them to the Lord

Let us give thanks to the Lord our God.
It is right to give God thanks and praise.

Creator God,
in whose garden our story began;
we praise and bless you for your continued
nurture and care as we grow in your kingdom.
We thank you for Jesus, who through his life,
death and resurrection opened the way
to fullness of life.
With angels and archangels, and all
who share in your life-giving love,
we praise you, singing
Holy, holy, holy is the Lord
Holy is the Lord God Almighty, (*repeat*)
Who was, and is, and is to come,
Holy, holy, holy is the Lord.

Come to us now, holy God,
as we remember Jesus,
who on the night before he died
took bread and wine, blessed them
and gave them to his friends, saying
Eat and drink to remember me.
Come freshly to us now, Lord God,
and bless these gifts of bread and wine.
As we receive them, may we be
rooted and grounded more deeply
in your love;

Nourish us with your life-giving Spirit,
and bring us at last to our full flowering,
where we shall glorify you for ever:
Glory, glory, glory to the Lord,
Glory to the Lord God almighty, (*repeat*)
Who was, and is, and is to come,
Glory, glory, glory to the Lord.

Ann Lewin

A Grace Before or After a Meal

Jesus Lord, bless this meal,
Guide and love us for ever.

Tune: Edelweiss

Pax Christi

After Meals

Glory to God for His good things.
Glory to God for His blessings.
Glory to God who has sustained us with His gifts.
Glory to God who has nourished us.
Glory to God who has satisfied us.
Glory to God by whose will we are alive.
Glory to God who is merciful.
May His mercies be upon us by the prayers of the mother of
    God
Mary and all the saints for ever and ever.
Amen.

Syrian Orthodox Church

A Meal Blessing

Blessed are you, Almighty Father,
for giving us our daily bread.
Blessed is Jesus, your beloved Son,
who continually feeds us on the Word of Life.
Blessed is the Holy Spirit
who unites us in love at this table.
We thank you for this food we have to eat
and ask that, in your goodness,
you will provide
for our sisters and brothers
who are hungry.
Amen.

Pax Christi

Small Grace

Dear Lord . . .
We beg you fortify us with this gift of food
That we may stronger strive to work for good,
That we may be empowered from above
To toil steadfastly, nourished by your love.
Amen.

Margot Arthurton

Secular Grace

Let us not,
Amidst our cases, and our causes,
And our haste
To fight the whole world's wrongs
In one swift blow,
Fail to give thanks
For water sweet to drink

And simple food—
Both do we need to fortify our lives
That we may stronger grow,
And so sustain
Our efforts for the common good.

Margot Arthurton

Waste Not, Want Not

Out of my abundance I choose to offer my gift,
knowing that what I regard as excess,
others may need, and all that I need,
others may regard as excess.

I choose not to waste,
so that others will not want,
and recognize that when all share,
all are enriched.

Lord take this gift and use it for your purpose.
Amen.

Christian Aid

Help Us to Care

Dear God
We know that the food we eat and drink
is grown by people far away.
Even though we will never meet them,
help us to care for their needs as well as our own.

Christian Aid

Grace

Give us, we pray, a loftier view of life
That we may watch the Earth
Upon its axis turn—
That we may not forget
How rains may flow to flood
And sun relentless burn . . .
And harvests fail . . .

Thus may we now give thanks
For all Earth's goodness set
Before us here–

And in this moment's quiet space
Together met,
We beg that you, who generous gives,
Accept our simple, humble grace.
Amen.

Margot Arthurton

Psalm of Praise

Adapted from Psalm 104

Leader: Praise the Lord, your God, my soul,
All: **God of all, how great you are**.
Leader: All the earth depends on you,
All: **God of all, how great you are**.
Leader: Crops for harvest, homes for shelter,
All: **God of all, how great you are**.
Leader: Bread for hunger. Oil for gladness,
All: **God of all, how great you are**.

Leader:	May your glory last for ever,
All:	**God of all, how great you are**.
Leader:	May our lives and worship please you,
All:	**God of all, how great you are**.

Christian Aid

A Maasai Prayer

Lord, sweeten the waters
Lord, sweeten the grass
Lord, sweeten and swell all the rivers
Lord, thicken all forests
Lord, sweeten all animals.

Lord, give us land
Lord, let the land be green
Lord, give us rains
Lord, give us fruitful lands
Lord, sweeten all rivers.

Kenya
Christian Aid and CAFOD

Charge Us with Power

May the God who breathes life into the broken,
who exposes our divisions and our pride,
whose tenderness is the strength of the poor,
bless us and charge us with power
to live as community in our world,
in the name of Christ.
Amen.

Christian Aid

Five Blessings from the Community of the Servants of the Will of God

Blessing of Beehives

Blessed are you, Lord God,
who in these your creatures,
the bees,
grant us a living example of industry
and unity of purpose.
Pour down your blessing upon them;
curb their desire to swarm;
grant them freedom from disease
and abundance of nectar in the blossom,
that by the sweet savour of their honey
we may bless you in the joy of festal days.
Glory to you. O Lord, glory to you.
Amen.

Blessing of Chickens

Blessed are you, Lord God,
for you have created these birds for our use.
Protect them from disease,
and prosper the work of our hands
that we may bless you again in the fruits of your bounty
through Christ our Lord.
Amen.

Blessing of the Herd of Cows

All praise and thanksgiving be to you,
Heavenly Father,
that you have entrusted this herd of cows to our care.

Protect them from disease and every kind of harm
and grant that as we enjoy their produce
we may bless your Holy Name,
through Jesus Christ our Lord.
Amen.

Blessing of the Fields

Blessed are you, O God,
for you have commanded your servants to replenish the earth
  and subdue it.
Direct now, O Lord, our work on these fields,
that your holy command and purpose
may be fulfilled in us;
through Christ our Lord.
Amen.

Blessing of the Garden Field

Almighty God,
you have created and blessed the earth
that it may supply our needs:
bless now, we beseech you,
this field, granting seasonable weather for growth
and health
to those who labour to your honour and glory;
through Christ our Lord.
Amen.

Community of the Servants of the Will of God

Blessing the Plants, Vines, Olives and Fruit Trees

O Creator God, who by your loving kindness created man
and gave him authority to cultivate the land, and ordered that
whatever we do we shall do it in your holy name, bless,
O Lord, by your mercies this place and these plants which

253

we sowed in your holy name. Make their roots firm, their tender twigs green, and keep them from blight, weevil, creeping locust and worms. Prove them to be plants of excellent shoots and rich in fruits that will gladden the hearts of the gardeners and those who grow them. May they produce crops of praise and thanksgiving to those who eat their fruits and are nourished by them, so that all of us may offer you glory and praise, for ever. Amen.

Syrian Orthodox Church

Blessing of Household Crops

Your right hand, O Lord, blessed a few loaves of bread in the wilderness and four thousand men, women and children did eat and were satisfied. Your right hand likewise blessed, through the prophet Elijah, a handful of flour in a pot and a little oil in a jar in the house of the widow. Even now, O Lord, stretch out your mighty right hand with mine who am your weak servant and bless these crops and this house. And as you blessed the dwelling and the household of the just of ancient times – Abraham, Isaac, Jacob, Joseph, Job and David – likewise, multiply your blessing on these crops of your worshippers so that, from our mouths, glory be raised to you now and for ever and ever. Amen.

Syrian Orthodox Church

Blessing Dried and Fresh Fruits

O God, who by your wisdom created the various kinds of fruit and all the different types of crops for the sustenance of human life, bless by your right hand that is full of gifts the variety of these fruits that have been prepared for us. Make them, O Lord, a source of physical nourishment and spiritual healing for all those who are sustained by them, Father, Son and Holy Spirit now and for ever. Amen.

Syrian Orthodox Church

Blessing a Market or Workshop

O Lord our God, who are the fountain of all good things, bless this building and the contents therein. Bless all those who work in it and keep them by your holy angels from all spiritual and physical injuries. Free them from severe temptation and grievous calamities. Make your abundant blessings to greatly enrich their properties. May they exceedingly flourish in all good things so that when their profits increase, likewise, their good works may be multiplied. Grant, O Lord, that they may worship your holy name, love one another sincerely and inherit everlasting life with all who were well pleasing to your will, Father, Son and Holy Spirit, now and for ever and ever. Amen.

Syrian Orthodox Church

Blessing of Springs and Wells

O Supreme Power, who in the beginning ordered the waters to gather in one place and become pools for the irrigation of your creation, bless, O Lord, these waters by your grace and mercy. Remove from them all injuries and harms and make them a source of health and help in time of distress to all those who use them so that your name may be glorified for ever. Amen.

Syrian Orthodox Church

Blessing of Seeds Before They are Sown

O Merciful God, bless by your grace these seeds and the house from which they come forth. May they be multiplied some thirty, some sixty and some a hundred fold. May they be sown with gladness, reaped with cheerfulness and gathered with exultation. May the threshing floors abound in grain and the granaries overflow with crops so that offerings of thanksgiving be offered to you who accept the offering of faithful

255

believers. May the needy be nourished with their harvest and the hungry be satisfied by their produce; then they will offer you praise, O Good Preserver, who supports the whole creation, Father, Son and Holy Spirit, now and for ever and ever. Amen.

Syrian Orthodox Church

Remember the Rainbow

We praise you God for your whole spectrum of colours.

For red, reminding us of the blood of Christ
For orange, reminding us of the fruits of the earth
For yellow, reminding us of the sun, giving us light and heat
For green, reminding us of all living things
For blue, reminding us of the sea and the sky
For indigo, reminding us of the dyes we use to colour the
    world
For violet, reminding us of flowers and trees.

For these and all the other colours that we see around us,
we praise you, God.
Amen.

Alan Baldwin

Lead Us to a New Awareness

May the good Lord lead us from this place
and take us to where he is living;
May he lead us to a new awareness of the poor
and show us his home among them;
May he lead us to a new desire for justice
and give us a glimpse of the kingdom he is building;
May he fill our hearts with generosity
and anoint us to be bearers of good news;
May his blessing be upon us as it is upon the poor,
and may he show us what he wants us to do.
Amen.

Christian Aid

Harvest Offering

*Receive the harvest offertory in jars to illustrate that God's people
have a part to play in the cycle of his provision. Put a single coin into
each jar. Pass the jars through the congregation so that people can
make a donation to the work of Christian Aid. Every person who
gives symbolically 'multiplies' the one coin in the jar.*

*Afterwards take the jars to the front of the church and pour the
money they contain into one central pot. The closer the pot comes to
spilling over, the better! Alternatively group all the jars together on
a central table. Then read together the offertory prayer:*

In your provision for our own needs,
we thank you.
In your desire to provide for the needs of all,
we honour you.
Let a full measure of provision flow,
to meet the needs of all God's people.
Amen.

Christian Aid

When the Time Comes

When the seasons of my life
have been completed,
when the time comes
for the harvest to be gathered in,
may the fruit of my labours
and my living and loving
be pleasing to you,
my heavenly Father.

Susan Hardwick

Christ Jesus is the Gardener

So many gifts of flowers, fruit and veg
The table's overflowing—
Wherever's it all going?

The children's Mums and Dads
Have raided pantry,
Cabbage patch and supermarket store—
To show a harvest richly blest
With loaves and fish – and all the best
Of gardeners' skills and florists' art
As each one plays their part.

So many care enough
That others may receive—
The homeless, sick or housebound,
We're all equal in God's eyes.
We each need the other;
Christ Jesus is the Gardener—
Desiring all to care and share each day
So prayers can find an answer!

Wendy Whitehead

Thanksgiving

Based on Mother Julian

For lambs that leap
and birds that sing,
for every blessed glorious thing
that God has made
and loves and keeps,
we thanks and praises bring.

Each smile exchanged,
new thoughts, sweet dreams,
for every blessed glorious thing
that God has made
and loves and keeps
we thanks and praises bring.

For Jesus Christ
our loving friend,
made, loved and kept
that we may sing
praises to our glorious King,
we thanks and worship bring.

Kate McIlhagga

O Glorious God

O Glorious God,
the whole creation proclaims your marvellous work:
increase in us a capacity to wonder and delight in it,
that heaven's praise may echo in our hearts
and our lives be spent as good stewards of the earth.
Through Jesus Christ our Lord.
Amen

Michael Townroe

Justice-Dealing God

Justice-dealing God,
we thank you for your grace and gifts;
and for your giving of yourself.

May we share all the gifts of your creation
– our living space with those who seek asylum
– our beliefs with those who have few or none
– our money with those who are hopelessly in debt
– and our food resources with those who are malnourished.

Bless our meal,
and our journeying
day by day
in the pilgrimage of faith.

Pamela Turner

Blessing an Abundant Harvest

Place many harvest symbols on the altar

Let us extend our hands over these harvest symbols and pray:

Blessed are you, Creator and Sustainer of All. We thank you for the gifts of an abundant harvest. They are symbols of our creative energy, the energy and newness of Spring which deepens and matures in Autumn. We thank you for the strength and the labour of women we have known: home-makers, office workers, farmers, gardeners, and all who labour, women whose muscle and mind move our world and speak of the power of women.

Let us bless these symbols by remembering women who sweat and toil for liberation and equality. Let us speak their names. (*Share the names*)

Diann Neu
USA

Blessing Apples

Blessed are you, Creator of All. We thank you for the apples we share. They are the fruit of the harvest, symbol of the fullness and ripeness of Autumn. We thank you for the ripeness of the women and men we have known, those who speak out in wisdom against all that holds us back from fullness.

Let us bless these apples by remembering the names of the ripe women and men in our lives: our mothers and fathers, grandparents, wise ones who birth, nurture, guide and love us. Let us speak their names. (*Share the names*)

Diann Neu
USA

Blessing Cider*

Blessed are you, Lover of All. We thank you for the cider we toast with and share. It comes from the fruits of Summer, a symbol of the joy and warmth of that season. We thank you for the passion and joy of those we have known: children and adolescents, those who celebrate all that yearns for completion.

Let us bless this drink by remembering our friends, daughters and sons, nieces and nephews, teachers and students, those who share their passion for life with the world. Let us speak their names. (*Share the names*)

Let us share these apples and cider remembering our harvest.

Diann Neu
USA

* Apple cider is a non-alcoholic drink made from the new season's crop in America and Canada.

Blessing of One Another

Let us put our arms around one another as we pray:

Blessed are you, Mother of All. We thank you for our selves, the greatest gifts we share with one another. We are the symbols of your warmth, caring, power, and wisdom.

We thank you for all the people who have touched our lives and revealed you to us: those who listen to us, who hear us, who counsel us, who heal us, people whose concern and support call us to an abundant harvest.

Let us bless one another by remembering friends who see visions of what can be and share that with us: seers, activists, creative spirits. Let us speak their names. (*Share the names*)

And let us embrace one another and send one another forth with a harvest greeting.

Diann Neu
USA

Seedtime and Harvest

God of yesterday, today and tomorrow,
God of seedtime and harvest,
Father, Son and Holy Spirit,
bless us and strengthen us
to live and blossom and bear good fruit
to his praise and glory.

Dorothy Stewart

A Blessing

Son of the living God,
shine upon us with your unfailing grace.
Grant us wisdom,
the power of faith
and unchanging hope.
Amen.

Ethiopian Orthodox Church

Sending Forth

I who am the source of all life, I send you forth
to manifest life for all the Earth.
Blessed be life.
Blessed be life.

I who am the beauty of all life, I send you forth
to manifest beauty for all the Earth.
Blessed be beauty.
Blessed be beauty.

I who am the power of all life, I send you forth
to manifest power for all the Earth.
Blessed be power.
Blessed be power.

I who am the truth of all life, I send you forth
to manifest truth for all the Earth.
Blessed be truth.
Blessed be truth.

I who am the energy of all life, I send you forth
to manifest energy for all the Earth.
Blessed be energy.
Blessed be energy.

Diann Neu
USA

Take Generous Blessings

Leave this Harvest Worship
knowing the richness of Harvest Blessings through
the Love of God,
      the Selfless-Giving of Christ,
            the Bounty of the Holy Spirit
      in your lives,
so that you can take generous blessings
to your neighbours in this local community;
send generous blessings
to your partners in global situations
so that they all may
know Peace.
Go with Shalom.
Amen.

Geoffrey Duncan

Part Eight:

Supplement of new material

'Not to enable the poor to share in our goods is to steal from them and deprive them of life. The goods we possess are not ours, but theirs.'

St John Chrysostom

God of All Creation

God of all light and colour, we praise you for the glories of red and yellow, green and gold and all the many shades of this harvest season.
We thank you for red apples, purple grapes and green cabbages,

> for oranges and lemons, peas and barley,
> beans and beetroot
> and the great variety of fruit and vegetables from
> harvests around the world.

We may not have had a hand in growing them, but we appreciate the dedication and hard work of the people who do.

The harvest of the earth is easily recognisable and a joy to all.

Yet your harvests are far more wide-ranging than these.

God of all creation, we would thank you for the creative powers of others:

> for intelligent and logical minds working on solutions
> to problems;
> for engineers and inventors, designers and mechanics,
> advisers and teachers;
> for artists and musicians, writers and performers,
> cooks and craft workers.

The harvest of creativity is so wide because you have given each of us the ability to be creative.

God of all love, we would thank you for the harvest of caring;
for doctors, nurses, the ambulance, police and fire and
rescue services;
for workers in the power and water industries,
and for all who work to serve us day by day;
for charity and welfare workers,
those who work for justice and freedom
and those who challenge us to have a conscience.

God of so many harvests, we struggle to include all our
gratitude in one prayer.
Help us to live our lives in appreciation of all that your life
offers to us.

Marjorie Dobson

This is Our Prayer

At harvest time we thank you, God,
For all the bounty we receive;
The planted seed, the growth of food
Are more than we alone achieve:
So may we always be aware
You give us life –
This is our prayer.

You give abundantly to us,
May we express our thanks to you
By giving freely of ourselves –
Our time, our talents, money too:
So may we learn to love, and share
The things we have –
This is our prayer.

The fruits of earth are meant for all,
For all are children who depend
Upon the need for food and clothes –

We sense the purpose you intend:
So may we pay what's just and fair
For others' work –
This is our prayer.

The earth you give us for our needs
Is not a place to waste and spoil,
We are but stewards of your world;
In trust – the seas, the air and soil:
So may we use with thought and care
Your planet earth –
This is our prayer.

The harvest of our hearts and minds
Will be the fruit of all we sow,
And many are the tares and weeds,
Yet blades of love and truth can grow:
God of the harvest, you are there,
Help us to grow –
This is our prayer.

Cecily Taylor

So Many Gifts . . .

So many gifts of flowers, fruit and veg.
The table's overflowing –
Wherever's it all going?

The children's Mums and Dads
Have raided pantry,
Cabbage patch and supermarket store –
To show a harvest richly blest
With loaves and fish – and all the best
Of gardeners' skills, and florists' art
As each one plays their part.

So many care enough –
That others will receive –
The homeless, sick or housebound,
We're all equal in God's eyes.
We each one need the other;
Christ Jesus is the gardener –
Desire all to care and share each day
So prayers can find an answer!

Wendy Whitehead

Prayer of Dedication of a Basket

A basket filled with food from developing countries should be placed centrally in the church.

Leader (*holding up the basket*):
This basket belongs to all and to no one.
It is the work of human hands.

Woven together to contain the good things of creation,
which are bought and sold in the market place.
As we dedicate it today,
we remember the hopes and dreams
of all who work to fill it,
and we pray for all those
whose lives may be nourished by its contents.

The paths we have been walking separately,
have brought us here together today,
to this moment,
when, though many, we are one.

We bless this basket and dedicate it to God's glory.
In the name of the Father who cares for us,
In the name of the Son who inspires us,
In the name of the Spirit who walks with us.

May it be a symbol
of our unity on this journey,
with those who labour, farm and toil.
And a sign
of the hospitality of God's banquet,
where a table is set for all peoples to share.
Amen.

Sophie Stanes
CAFOD

Come to the Fiesta

Come, come, come to the fiesta,
Come to dance
and come to sing;
though we're poor it doesn't matter,
share your food,
share everything.
Let's denounce the cruel oppression,
let no one be king
and no one slave;
sharing our lives
and hearts
and fortune
is our Christian way of life.

Vamos Caminando
Peru

The Land is a Gift from God

We believe that the land is a gift from God. God is the owner
of the land and humans are only stewards to look after it.
Human beings are created from the dust of the earth – we are
part of the land and if the land is misused it will have an ad-
verse effect on humanity. Human beings have a responsibility
to use the land in a sustainable manner. But the processes of

globalisation are geared to work against the biblical concept of land. Land must not be viewed merely as a geographical entity but as a living entity.

We must begin to undertake a sacrificial sharing of affluence – it is through solidarity that the common good can be achieved. Mere rhetoric is not enough – words and intentions have to be translated into action. In the Christian world there is no forum to challenge the affluent and point out extravagant living. We need to make effective changes so that the gap between the rich and the poor may be reduced.

Fr Reid Shelton Fernando
CAFOD
Sri Lanka

The One Who Produces

If the poor didn't plant
what would the rich do?
They have money in their pockets
but that doesn't produce food.
The person who walks barefoot
is the one who produces
in order to see Brazil* grow.

Jose Costa Leite
Brazil

* *Other countries' names or more than one country may be inserted here.*

You Were Obese

I was hungry and starving and you were obese;
Thirsty, and you were watering your garden;
With no road to follow
    and without hope
        and you called the police
            and were happy that they took me prisoner.

Barefoot and with ragged clothing and you were saying:
>'I will buy something new.'

Sick and you asked:
>'Is it infectious?'

Prisoner and you said:
>'That is where all those of your class should be.'

Lord, have mercy!

Author Unknown
CAFOD

Food and Hunger

Human dignity implies the need to protect each person. For this reason food is not the right only of those who have purchasing power, or those who produce – it is the right of every human being. The right to life requires distributive justice and it stands above the criteria of the market. Nobody should be fearful of falling into poverty or of going hungry. Food security implies the quantity, quality, continuity and suitability of food to cultural customs. Food is not to be treated as one merchandise among others, which is produced and accumulated according to the interests of its owners. As long as human beings are going hungry, it is immoral to stock food to guarantee speculative profits.

Brazilian Bishops' Conference
CAFOD

Give Us Today Our Daily Bread

Generous, loving God we ask you
To give us today our daily bread.
Creator of the world we share
Give us today our daily bread
As we store the crops
And fill the barns
Stack the shelves

Pile high the tins
And wander the aisles
Of supermarket choice
Show us how to see the world
Through the eyes of the hungry
Teach us how to share with all
Our daily bread.

Linda Jones
CAFOD

Blessing of Food for Shared Meal or Picnic

Generous, loving God we ask you
To give us today our daily bread.
Creator of the world we share
Give us today our daily bread.
Show us how to see the world
Through the eyes of the hungry
Teach us how to share with all
This daily bread.
Amen.

Sophie Stanes
CAFOD

Dare to Hope

We dare to imagine a world,
Where hunger has no chance to show its face.
We dare to dream of a world,
Where war and terror are afraid to leave their mark.
We long to believe in a world,
Of hope unchained and lives unfettered.
We dare to share in the creation of a world,
Where your people break free.

Dare we open our minds to difference?
Dare we open our lives to change?

Your kingdom come, O Lord
Your will be done
Amen.

Linda Jones
CAFOD

Build and Plant

Holy God, as you plucked up the people of Israel
And set them down to build and to plant,
So stretch out your life-giving hand to the dispossessed,
That with our help they may build and plant,
Reap and sow, dance and sing.
Fill them with courage to love,
Strength to rebuild and grace to grow,
That once more they may rise up and cry freedom,
May shake off the chains of oppression to wear dignity,
And may leave behind the shackles of despair
To embrace hope.

Annabel Shilson-Thomas
CAFOD

A Feast for All

Loving God,
We gaze in wonder
At the splendour of your creation.
We see a banquet spread before us,
Rich carpeted fields of yellowing grain
And overflowing baskets of ripe fruit.
We see a banquet prepared for all peoples,
Of fine wines and rich food
A generous feast for all to share.

Linda Jones
CAFOD

Prawn Farming in Bangladesh

Ambika's Story

Ambika lives in a coastal village in Bangladesh. She works as a wage labourer, building embankments around prawn ponds, maintaining roads and weeding the fields. She also earns cash by helping to clean and pack harvested prawns, but this work is seasonal and poorly paid and she has less time for her traditional unpaid work in family farming and household duties.

Cultivating prawns provides work for women like Ambika in areas where living standards are extremely low. Her income has given her some economic independence but other women complain that they are sexually harassed by men and despised by villagers who feel women should not work outside the home. Because of this disrespect, her family may have difficulty in finding her a husband.

Prawn farms provide work for men in the construction of embankments, roads and buildings, but once these are completed the work, is over.

Ambika's brother is employed as a security guard but many men have to leave the area to find work because traditional ways of working the land have disappeared. Ambika's little sister can also earn money – she often spends long hours waist-high in water collecting prawn fry. It is unpleasant, back-breaking work and the low pay does not make up for the reduction in family income caused by the advent of prawn farming.

Aquaculture has been a mixed blessing to Ambika's family, the community and the region where they live.

Christian Aid

They Lost Their Livelihoods

The Nilgiri Hills of Tamil Nadu are a very poor region in southern India, characterised by low-quality land and limited employment opportunities. The tribal communities (*adivasis*) who populate the region live a marginalised existence, earning a subsistence income from the collection and sale of non-timber forest products such as berries, fruits and honey.

Although the *adivasis* are experienced forest managers who encourage bio-diversity and sustainability in their collection of forest produce, their already precarious existence suffered further when the government introduced a policy of auctioning produce collection licences to the highest bidder. *Adivasis*, being unable to offer a high bid, lost their livelihoods. Many were forced to seek work on a seasonal basis for exploitative wages or had to leave the area altogether.

As a consequence *adivasis* have lived in extreme poverty with widespread malnutrition and disease, high infant mortality, low life expectancy and lack of basic necessities such as safe water for domestic use.

However, the establishment of community-based Adivasis Forest Produce Societies has empowered them to encourage an awareness of collective strength and community self-reliance. Successful campaigning has brought an end to licence auctions and secured the *adivasis'* right to collection of forest produce and the recognition that they are the best people to sustainably manage and protect the forests.

Since winning back their rights, they have started to process and market gooseberry and borams, which are made into pickles; gallnuts are crushed into powder and used in ayurvedic and holistic medicine; tamarind is dried, packaged and sold for culinary purposes; tree moss is scraped from trees and sold for culinary purposes; honey is produced for sale in local and urban markets and soap nuts are used as an alternative to soap.

Demand for forest produce is growing, and with continued training and support the *adivasis* will generate an income that is significant enough for collection to become a self-supporting sustainable livelihood.

Living standards will continue to improve, with participants being able to pay off long-term debts or purchase food, school books and household items.

Poverty is being reduced by creating greater economic independence, increasing food security and improving health, nutrition and living conditions.

Find Your Feet

Our Strength and Our Help

Living God,
Our strength and our help.
We turn to you in our distress.
May the spirit of compassion
Comfort and protect your people.

In the parched lands and failed harvests
We see you hungry.
May the shadow of that hunger
Be broken by the light of your hope.

In our hearts we hold a vision
Of a better world.
May we, by our actions,
Bear witness to your love.

Linda Jones
CAFOD

Trade for Life

Kalayaan's Story

Kalayaan, whose name means 'freedom', is eleven years old and lives on Mindoro, one of the islands in the Philippines. His ambition is to be a fisherman like his father and grandfather, taking his small boat out every day to catch fresh fish to eat and sell in the market.

An international company wants to start mining nickel in the hills behind the bay, cutting down trees and taking water from the rivers to wash nickel out of the ground. It will refine the nickel using chemicals, and polluted waste water will be piped out to sea, killing the fish on which the people depend. The mining company tells them they will be paid good money and they will all get rich. What will happen when all the nickel has been taken? The company will leave, the land and sea will be ruined; there will be no job, no money and no fish for Kalayaan to catch.

With the help of a local organisation called MAHAL, the people protest to the government as well as to the mining company. They are poor people on a tiny island where there is wealth in the ground. Who is going to listen to them and who decides in a case like this? What is the decision based upon?

Governments often badly need the extra money that big international companies can bring; the company wants the financial profits from the business, yet it is the local people whose lives will be most directly affected.

What effect does their protest have?

Christian Aid

Reflection on the Scales of Justice

Our choice could
tip the balance
in favour of the poor
and lighten the load
of those weighed down

We could level inequality
and distribute warehouse mountains
share out the wealth
that was never ours to hoard

279

Turn the tables
on those who play
the markets

We could stockpile generosity
and speculate in hope
Sell up our shares in selfishness
and settle for the dividends
of solidarity

For added value
build portfolios of justice
or an ISA in the growth
of the kingdom of God
Buy shares in trust and act in faith
risk our securities to find a richer life

May the percentage of our interest
in people rise
and may we be the prophets
of hope.

Sophie Stanes
CAFOD

Open Our Eyes to Fairness

Lord,
Open our eyes to the need for fairness,
Open our eyes to the cries of the people.
Open our hearts to a greater understanding,
Open our lips to share the truth.

Give us the courage to speak out.
Give us the confidence to confront the powerful.
Give us the strength to persevere.
Be with us, Lord, as we strive to create a fairer world.

Kathleen Scullion
CAFOD

Money Comes before Christian Values

At the moment money rules life . . . money comes before Christian values. Through a spirit of co-operation we can make trade work for everyone. The idea must be that my profit is not only my profit but the fruit of everyone's labours.

Father George Anastacio
CAFOD
Mozambique

Trade and the Economy

The integration of the poorer economies into an equitable world trade system is in the interest of all. The enhanced development of the poorer countries is a contribution to global progress, international security and peace. In a globalised economy no one can be insensitive to the situation of those who are lingering on its margins. Inclusiveness is both a moral and an economic value.

Archbishop Diarmuid Martin
CAFOD
Doha

Ethical Trade and Equity

We believe in ethical trade.
We believe in fair rules for trade.
We believe in equity –
that the same rules for all are not necessarily just.
'The big people in the World Trade Organisation want a level playing field – the tigers and the rabbits in the same cage.'

Sarath Fernando
CAFOD
Sri Lanka

We Pray for the Church Throughout the World (1)

We pray for the Church throughout the world, that we may
demonstrate to the world a living, vibrant faith,
which seeks to include and share, and speaks out against
the scandal of poverty.

We pray for world leaders, that they may listen to the
voices of those who live in poverty and begin to use their
power generously for the good of all.

We pray for ourselves, that through our choices, action
and words we may live out our faith in our everyday lives,
growing more compassionate and generous each day.

Linda Jones
CAFOD

We Pray for the Church Throughout the World (2)

We pray for the Church throughout the world, that it may
be a living example of a loving community and a voice for
those who are hungry for food and justice.

We pray for the world's leaders, that they may work to
overcome the barriers between people and foster a spirit
of global community in a world where no one has to
experience poverty or hunger.

We pray for ourselves, that we may have the courage to
be witnesses to the power of sharing and to the values of
global community.

Linda Jones
CAFOD

The Way of God

The way of God lies deep within
The mystic Christ declares –
A journey to a wondrous feast
Which God, with love, prepares.
The journey centres on the choice
Between the many ways
Of leaving lesser things behind
To have a life of praise.

The lesser self attends our needs
For shelter and for food
But by itself it only brings
A surface vein of good.
It is the deeper Godlike self
Which brings both peace and grace
A sense that where we live our lives
Is truly sacred space.

When we exceed the balanced way
Consuming others' shares
The starving poor, on dying earth
Confirm our nightmare fears.
Unless we walk the inner way
The surface-self will rule –
Our greed will overtake our need
And kill our holy fool.

The path of Christ brings sacrifice –
A costly letting go,
A willingness of painful choice
Beyond the space we know;
But when we walk with fearless hearts
And wisdom we can own
We find each pilgrim resting place
Becomes our sacred home.

William L .Wallace
Aotearoa New Zealand

I Dare to Pray: Lord, Let the World be Changed

I dare to pray: Lord, let the world be changed,
for I long to see the end of poverty;
I dare to pray: Lord, let the rules be changed,
for I long to see trade bring justice to the poor;
I dare to pray: Lord, let my life be changed,
for I long to bring hope where good news is needed.
In the strength of your Spirit
and inspired by your compassion,
I make this promise to work for change,
and wait confidently for the day
when you make all things new.

Peter Graystone

God of Peace

God of peace,
Today in the wilderness
Springs beauty like water
Seeds lie in the dry earth
Awaiting the rains
Where parched desert cracked,
will flow mighty rivers
In a garden of plenty
Trees yield up their fruit
Together in your love
We will realise our tomorrow
With all those who scattered,
Gather our crops
In farms, field and cities
We will celebrate your justice
And in loving community
Reap a harvest of hope.

Linda Jones
CAFOD

284

Harvest Supper Recipes

These recipes first appeared in a Christian Aid publication and can be easily adapted for Church harvest festivals and other occasions.

Ethiopian Recipes

Meals in Ethiopia are a time for sharing and giving. The most popular dishes are stews called wo'ts which are usually served on a giant pancake called injera. Wo'ts can also be served with rice, bread, salads, humous and dhals. Here are some recipes for you to savour.

Injera

Makes 25 pancakes

Injera pancakes are a staple part of Worknesh's diet in Ethiopia. They are tasty and easy to make, but unfortunately don't require tossing – injera is only cooked on one side! Once you have cooked your pancakes, let them cool down and serve two per person – one laid out flat on the plate and the other on top folded in half like a napkin. In Ethiopia you use your right hand to tear off the pancake and use it instead of knives and forks to scoop up your stews and salads.

Ingredients

6 g of dried yeast
500 g of brown or plain white flour
warm water

Method

Mix the dry ingredients together in a bowl, stir and add a little water so that the injera mixture is a little runny. Cover with a tea towel and leave somewhere warm overnight. When you are about to cook, give the mixture a good stir and add a little water to get a pancake-mixture consistency. Heat the frying pan and add a ladle of injera mixture, tilting the pan in a circular motion so that the mixture lies flat in the pan. Wait for the injera to change colour, then cover for 20 seconds. Remove cover and use the spatula to lift the injera to slide it onto a plate.

Doro w'ot/Chicken Stew

Serves 5

A spicy chicken dish which is a bright red colour.

Ingredients

1 large chicken
(allow 250 g per person)
3 small onions, finely chopped
1 hot red chilli pepper, deseeded and finely chopped (replace with tomato paste for a mild dish)
50 g butter
1 crushed garlic clove (or a little garlic paste)
½ tsp chopped fresh ginger (or a pinch of ginger powder)
250 ml of water
6 hard-boiled eggs
1 lemon
salt and pepper

Method

Remove skin from chicken, rinse well and quarter. Quarter lemon and add to a large bowl of salty clean water and soak the chicken for an hour. Chop the onions, garlic and ginger and fry in the butter until golden. Then add the red chilli pepper (or tomato paste) and 125 ml of water. Dry the chicken

pieces and add them to the pan and cook for about 30–40 minutes stirring now and then and adding the rest of the water.
When the sauce begins to thicken, add the salt and pepper.
Cook and shell the hard-boiled eggs. Score the eggs lightly
and add to sauce for decoration.

Ye'atakllt Alich'a / Vegetable Stew

Serves 5

A mild steamed vegetarian dish which has a deep yellow
colour from the turmeric used in the recipe.

Ingredients

2 tbsp sunflower oil
3 small chopped onions
6 medium-sized potatoes
5 carrots
2 tsp turmeric
1 small cabbage
(or 1 small cauliflower / 1 stem of broccoli)
3 cloves of garlic
(or garlic paste)
1 deseeded green chilli pepper sliced lengthwise, for
    decoration
salt and pepper to taste

Method

Cut the onions in thick chunks and cook in the oil until golden.
Add the crushed garlic cloves or paste. Add the turmeric and
mix well. Meanwhile peel and slice carrots in thick chunks so
they don't dissolve when cooking, cut cabbage into large
pieces and add them to the onions. Stir gently and cook until
tender. Peel and cut potatoes in chunks (use a potato peeler to
round off any sharp edges) and add to the pot. Lower the heat,

add a little water and cover the pot. Steam for 30 minutes or until the potatoes are cooked. Just before serving, arrange the slices of green chilli pepper on the dish and add salt and pepper.

Teemateem beqarya/Tomato and Green Pepper Salad

Serves 5

Ingredients

3 large fresh tomatoes
1 green chilli pepper (or sweet pepper)
1 small chopped onion
4 tbsp olive oil
4 tsp lemon juice or vinegar
Salt to taste
¼ tsp black pepper

Method

Wash tomatoes and chop into small pieces. Chop deseeded green pepper. Mix remaining ingredients in a bowl. Add the tomatoes to the mixture and toss gently. Serve immediately, with pitta bread and humous.

Indian Recipes

Cooking styles in India differ from one region to another. The dishes people cook also depend on their religion.

The blended spices which form the basis of Indian cooking create delicious flavours and aromas. Dhal is the Indian word for pulses such as lentils and beans. Over 50 different varieties of dhal are grown in India. Raitas are made by combining yoghurt with fresh vegetables. They go well with spicy food and have a cooling effect.

Pilau Rice

Serves 4–6

Ingredients

6 oz/150 g white long grain rice
2 oz/50 g butter
half an onion (chopped finely)
5 cloves
3 pods of cardamon
1 stick of cinnamon
½ tsp turmeric or a pinch of saffron
2 cups water

Method

Wash the rice thoroughly to get rid of starch. Soak it for half an hour. Heat the butter in a saucepan and fry the onion until lightly brown along with cloves, cardamons, cinnamon and turmeric. Add the washed rice and fry gently. Then pour in the water and bring to the boil. When water starts bubbling turn heat very low, cover pan with lid, leave for 15 minutes. Serve with dhal.

Dhal

Serves 6

Ingredients

6 oz/150 g red lentils (washed and soaked)
1 to 3 red chillies (to taste)
1 medium onion and 4 cloves garlic – all finely chopped
½ tsp cumin (use seeds if you can get them)
½ tsp turmeric powder
1½ tbsp coriander powder

salt to taste
4 oz/100 g unsalted butter

Method

Drain the lentils and cook in fresh water, using twice the amount of water to lentils. Add onion, chillies, cumin seeds, coriander and turmeric. Bring to the boil and leave to simmer until the lentils are soft and mushy (about 10 minutes). Add salt, boil for another couple of minutes, mix well. (The consistency should be like thick soup, so boil to get rid of excess water or add water as necessary.) Heat butter in a shallow pan and add garlic. Cook until brown and then add to the dhal mixture and stir gently. Serve hot with naan bread, rice or pitta bread.

Spiced Semolina Halva (biscuits)

Serves 6–8

Ingredients

5 fl oz/150 ml water
6 oz/175 g caster sugar
4 oz/100 g butter
4 oz/100 g semolina
4 oz/100 g seedless raisins
finely grated rind of one orange
2 oz/50 g ground almonds
6 whole green cardamons – skinned and crushed

Method

Put sugar and water in saucepan. Heat gently until sugar is dissolved. Bring to the boil and cook without stirring until syrup has thickened and reduced by half. Remove from heat. In a separate pan (such as a wok) melt the butter, add the semolina and cook until lightly browned, stirring constantly. Add the raisins, orange rind, ground almonds and crushed cardamons. Pour the syrup onto the semolina mixture and cook gently, stirring continuously until the mixture has thickened. Pour into a wetted 7 in/18 cm square cake tin. Allow to set. Cut into small squares. Serve as a sweet at your meal or with tea/coffee after your morning service.

An African Recipe

Groundnut Chicken

Serves 10

Ingredients

2 medium-sized chickens, cut into pieces
8 oz/225 g ground peanuts or 4 oz/200 g peanut butter
2 finely chopped onions
2 large sweet potatoes (ordinary potatoes will do)
salt and pepper to taste
chopped coriander leaves
2¼ lbs/1 kg rice (dry weight), boiled

Method

Simmer chicken pieces in enough water to cover them for half an hour. Add rest of ingredients, except for rice. Cover and simmer until the chicken and potatoes are tender. Add more water if needed. Serve over the hot rice.

Index of Authors and Sources

Index of Titles

Part One: For the beauty of the earth . . .

Part Two: Sharing in God's work

Part Three: 'Cursed is the ground . . .'

Part Four: Let me be as Christ to you . . .

Part Five: Summer and winter, and springtime and harvest . . .

Part Six: The harvest of the land and sea

Part Seven: Prayers, graces and blessings

Part Eight: Supplement of new material

Acknowledgements and Sources

Part One: For the beauty of the earth . . .

Affirmation of Faith © The Pacific Women's Consultation on Justice, Peace and the Integrity of Creation

As Keen as Mustard © Susan Hardwick, an Anglican priest and author of a number of books

Awareness © Alan Litherland

Beauty of Your Handiwork, The © W. L. Wallace

Butterfly © Pat Marsh

Celebrating the Uniqueness of Trees © Pax Christi, The Philippines

Coconut Tree © Sun-Ai Lee Park from *In God's Image*, and adapted, Vol. 18 No. 3 1999

Come, Come Away © Jerry Dan

Creation © Alan Litherland

Dreamer at Prayer © Wendy Whitehead

Gardener's Delight, A © The Uniting Church in Australia

God in Creation © Ruth Norton – Ravensthorpe United Reformed Church

God of the Whirlwind © Janet Lees

Harvest People © Frances Ballantyne

Jewel on the Cushion, The © Pat Marsh

Litany of Praise © Diann Neu, Co-Director of WATER, The Women's Alliance for Theology, Ethics and Ritual, 8035 13th Street, Silver Spring, MD20910, USA

Painted Flowers © Frances Ballantyne

Peace Trees © Ann Lewin

Praise God for Things that Grow © Elisabeth Cosnett

Praise You Lord © Christian Aid

Rainbow God © John Johansen-Berg

Respect for the Earth © Christian Aid

Rivers, Mountains and Trees © Garth Hewitt

St Francis © Ann Lewin

Seed, The © Margot Arthurton

Spirit of Creation and Community © Jan Berry

Statement of Faith © Christian Aid

Take a Look © Frances Ballantyne

Thanksgiving © The Arthur Rank Centre

Tree-Planting Liturgy, A © Zionist Bishop Reuben Marinda

We Belong to the Earth, © Sinfonia Oecumenica

You Who are in the Wind © The Society of Our Lady of the Isles

Part Two: Sharing in God's Work

Angel of the North, The © Alan Bell from *Magnet*, published by the Women's Network of the Methodist Church

Asebech's Family © Christian Aid

Care of the Earth, The © Christian Ecology Link

Co-creators of the Earth © Christian Aid and CAFOD

Creative Carelessness © Marjorie Dobson

Creator God © John Johansen-Berg

Divine Embroiderer © John Johansen-Berg

Earth is Our Mother, The © Christian Aid and CAFOD

Earth is the Lord's, The © Council for World Mission

Farming Community, The © The Arthur Rank Centre

Generosity © John Johansen-Berg

Heavenly Artist © John Johansen-Berg

In Times of Crisis © The Arthur Rank Centre

Our Ancestors Taught Us to Share © Christian Aid and CAFOD

Partners Together © Janet Lees

People Who Create © Bob Warwicker

Prayer by the Rose Arbour © Community of the Sisters of the Church

Prayer for Forgiveness © Christian Ecology Link

Prayer in the Orchard, Bible and Prayer Gardens © Community of the Sisters of the Church

Prayer in the Vegetable Garden © Community of the Sisters of the Church

Tenderness between People © Christian Aid

This Time of Crisis and Anxiety © The Arthur Rank Centre

Times of Distress in the Farming Community © The Arthur Rank Centre

Tools for Self-reliance © Kate McIlhagga

Part Three: 'Cursed is the ground . . .'

Acute Shortages © The Schumacher Centre

All-Seeing God © Geoffrey Duncan

. . . And It Was Very Good © Heather Pencavel

Banana Workers from Costa Rica © World Development Movement

Best of the Bunch? © Christian Aid

Cashew Crisis © Christian Aid

Climate Change © The Uniting Church in Australia

Dearth © Anne Richards

Divine Artist and Painbearer © W. L. Wallace

Drought © Margot Arthurton

Fisher Folk in Kerala © Christian Aid and CAFOD

Forest is our Livelihood, The © Declaration of the Penan Forest People, Borneo

From Dry Mass I © Brian Louis Pearce

From Dry Mass II © Brian Louis Pearce

Give, Act and Pray © Rebecca Dudley, Christian Aid

Giving © Margot Arthurton

Globalization © John Johansen-Berg

Harvest for the World © Geoffrey Duncan

Harvest Prayer of Confession © Alan Gaunt

Harvest Time © Jenny Dann

If the Land Could Speak © Kalinga

Importance of Clean Drinking Water, The © Commitment for Life, The
United Reformed Church

Justice and Compassion © Alan Litherland

Living Water © Heather Johnston

Lord of Life and Love © Geoffrey Duncan

Love your Neighbour © Jenny Dann

Modelling © Lindsey Sanderson

My Right Can Be Your Wrong © Susan Hardwick, an Anglican priest
and author of a number of books

Our Need for Water © Christian Aid and Geoffrey Duncan

Parable of the Bad Burger Bar Owner, The © Janet Lees

Peaceful Farmers © Christian Aid

Prayer of Confession © Diann Neu, Co-Director of WATER, The Water's
Alliance for Theology, Ethics and Ritual, 8035 13th Street, Silver
Spring, MD20910, USA

Prayers from the Countryside © Marlene Phillips

Puddles and Rainbows © Margot Arthurton

Quench Our Thirst © Christian Aid

Reflections © W. L. Wallace

Reflections on the Land © Christian Aid and CAFOD

Regeneration © W. L. Wallace

Rice or Pineapples? © Christian Aid

Simplistic? © Margot Arthurton

Sinned Against, The © Brian Louis Pearce

Sylvester is Four Years Old © Anthea Dove

Wendover © Brian Louis Pearce

What's It Worth? © Heather Pencavel

Words of Wisdom © Jan Berry

Vineyard Song © Jenny Dann

Part Four: Let me be as Christ to you . . .

Agnes © Christian Aid

All You Have Given © Jenny Dann

Beyond Fishing © World Council of Churches

Buyers and Sellers – Source Unknown

Change My Destiny © Christian Aid

Change My Ways © Angela Topping

Christ Our Advocate © Kate McIlhagga, from the Prayer Handbook 1993
published by the United Reformed Church

Christ, We Do Not Recognize, Andrew Pratt © Stainer and Bell

Coffee Grower's Comment, A © Miguel Barrantes

Collecting for Charity © Alan Baldwin

Compassionate Lord © Geoffrey Duncan

Creator and Provider © Alan Litherland

Crumbs of Cake © Frances Ballantyne

Dawning of Another Day, The © Peter Millar

Divine Redeemer © John Johansen-Berg

Enslaved by Debt, a Worldwide Grief, Andrew Pratt © Stainer and Bell

Fair Measure © Christian Aid

Favela, My Treasure © Christian Aid

Feed the Poor © W. L. Wallace

From the Cradle to the Grave © Christian Aid

Generous Hands © Christian Aid

Give Us This Day © Frances Ballantyne

God of Justice – Source Unknown

God of Liberation © W. L. Wallace

God's Generosity © Jan Berry

Great Feast of Life, The © Christian Aid

Harvest Festival © Anne Richards

Harvest Prayer © Alan Gaunt

Help Us Lord . . . © Moon Sharma, Tara Projects

Help Us to Grow Together, O God © The Uniting Church in Australia

I'm in Need © Frances Ballantyne

Impartial God from *Active Power, the Prayer Handbook 1998* © United Reformed Church

Inside Out © Margot Arthurton

Living with the New Economic Order © The Uniting Church in Australia

Lord of Life © Geoffrey Duncan

Making the Connection © Fiona Ritchie-Walker

Malnourished © United Nations Association

Many of Us Struggle to Lose Weight © Christian Aid and Philippa Harbin

Multi-Grain Bread of Life, The © Jeff Thompson

One Family © John Johansen-Berg

Our Father Who is in Us © Christian Aid

Peruvian Woman, A © Christian Aid

Praying for Change © Traidcraft

Put Love in the Heart © Fair Trade

Question of Judgement, A © Susan Hardwick, an Anglican priest and author of a number of books

Right to Health © John Johansen-Berg

Rukmani's Story: the Himalayas, North India © Christian Aid

School, Coffee and Squash © Christian Aid

Shared Interest © Shared Interest

Shivagami © Christian Aid

Some of Us © Pamela Turner

Stories about Coffee © Mario Hernandez, Robert Diaz, Carlos A. Vargas, Zacharia Kiwale

Part Five: Summer and winter, and springtime and harvest . . .

Pirouette © Brian Louis Pearce

Put People before Profit © Geoffrey Duncan

Seasoned Creation © Susan Hardwick, an Anglican priest and author of a number of books

Seasons © Janet Lees

Seedlings © Dhyanchand Carr

Sower, Nurturer, Winnower © Janet Lees

Spreading Hope © Christopher P. Burkett

Staple Diet in Ethiopia – Source Unknown

Summer's End © Pamela Turner

Terminology © Ann Lewin from *Flashes of Brightness*

Thoughts on an Early Morning Walk in Central Java © Pamela Ferguson

Worship for a Worldwide Harvest © Alan Bell from *Magnet* published by the Women's Network of the Methodist Church

You are the Life of the World © Ethiopian Orthodox Church

Part Six: The harvest of the land and sea

Agricultural Blacksmith, The © Christian Aid

Back-breaking Work © Christian Aid

Be Careful with the Earth's Gifts © Christian Aid

Behind and Within © W. L. Wallace

Blessing the Boats © Kate McIlhagga

By the Sweat of Your Brow You Shall Eat Your Food © Bob Warwicker

Complexity of Global Forces, The © Christopher P. Birkett

Day in the Life of a Breadmaker, A © Christian Aid

Eight Bowls of Dough © Christian Aid

Empowering Women © *Commitment for Life*, The United Reformed Church

Farmers' Festival © John Johansen-Berg

Farming Together © Christian Aid

Fingerling Cultivation © The Schumacher Centre

Fish Become Big Business © Christian Aid

For the Pressure of Work © Christopher P. Burkett

Fruits of Survival © Mohammad Aslam

Gather Round the Table © John Johansen-Berg

God, Maker and Breaker of Bread © Jan Berry

God of Resourcefulness © Geoffrey Duncan

God of Rice and Chapatti © Jenny Spouge

Growing Food for Survival: Ethiopia © Christian Aid

Harvest Eucharist © Duncan L. Tuck

Harvest of the Sea © Heather Johnston

Industrial Harvest, An © Heather Pencavel

Land of Gold © John Crocker

Litany of the Ocean, A © Bernard Thorogood

Major Indian Field Crops © Anil Kumar Patil

New Rice Fields and Fish Ponds © Christian Aid

On Practical Sharing © Muriel Orevillo-Montenegro

Paddy Fields © Alison Leishman

Prayer for the Harvests of Cereals, Pulses and Oils, A © Geoffrey Duncan

Response to God's Generosity, A © Claire Smith

Starvation within Harvest © Glenn Jetta Barclay

Thank Him © Norwyn Denny

Where Apples are Exotic Fruit © Christian Aid

Part Seven: Prayers, graces and blessings

After Meals © Syrian Orthodox Church

Blessing, A © Ethiopian Orthodox Church

Blessing a Market or Workshop © Syrian Orthodox Church

Blessing an Abundant Harvest © Diann Neu, Co-Director of WATER, The Women's Alliance for Theology, Ethics and Ritual, 8035 13th Street, Silver Spring, MD20910, USA

Blessing Apples © Diann Neu, Co-Director of WATER, The Women's Alliance for Theology, Ethics and Ritual, 8035 13th Street, Silver Spring, MD20910, USA

Blessing Cider © Diann Neu, Co-Director of WATER, The Women's Alliance for Theology, Ethics and Ritual, 8035 13th Street, Silver Spring, MD20910, USA

Blessing Dried and Fresh Fruits © Syrian Orthodox Church

Blessing of Household Crops © Syrian Orthodox Church

Blessing of One Another © Diann Neu, Co-Director of WATER, The Women's Alliance for Theology, Ethics and Ritual, 8035 13th Street, Silver Spring, MD20910, USA

Blessing of Seeds Before They Are Sown © Syrian Orthodox Church

Blessing of Springs and Wells © Syrian Orthodox Church

Blessing the Plants, Vines, Olives and Fruit Trees © Syrian Orthodox Church

Call to Worship © Kate McIlhagga

Charge Us with Power © Christian Aid

Christ Jesus is the Gardener © Wendy Whitehead

Dear God © Louisa Fenn

Eucharistic Blessing, A © Pax Christi

Eucharistic Prayer for a Quiet Garden Day © Ann Lewin

Five Blessings © Community of the Servants of the Will of God

Grace © Margot Arthurton

Grace Before or after a Meal, A © Pax Christi

Harvest Offering © Christian Aid

Help Us to Care © Christian Aid

Justice-Dealing God © Pamela Turner

Lead Us to a New Awareness © Christian Aid

Maasai Prayer, A © Christian Aid and CAFoD

Meal Blessing, A © Pax Christi

O Glorious God © Michael Townroe

Our Father Who is in Us © Christian Aid

Psalm of Praise © Christian Aid

Remember the Rainbow © Alan Baldwin

Secular Grace © Margot Arthurton

Seedtime and Harvest © Dorothy Stewart

Sending Forth © Diann Neu, Co-Director of WATER, The Women's Alliance for Theology, Ethics and Ritual, 8035 13th Street, Silver Spring, MD20910, USA

Small Grace © Margot Arthurton

Take Generous Blessings © Geoffrey Duncan

Thanksgiving © Kate McIlhagga

Waste Not, Want Not © Christian Aid

When the Time Comes © Susan Hardwick, an Anglican priest and author of a number of books

Part Eight: Supplement of new material

Blessing of Food for Shared Meal or Picnic © Sophie Stanes/CAFOD

Build and Plant © Annabel Shilson-Thomas/CAFOD

Come to the Fiesta © Vamos Caminando, from *Continent of Hope*

Dare to Hope © Linda Jones/CAFOD

Ethical Trade and Equity © Sarath Fernando

Feast for All, A © Linda Jones/CAFOD, from *Prayers for a Change*

Food and Hunger © Brazilian Bishops' Conference

Give Us Today Our Daily Bread © Linda Jones/CAFOD

God of All Creation, Marjorie Dobson © Stainer and Bell Ltd

God of Peace © Linda Jones/CAFOD

I Dare to Pray: Lord, Let the World Be Changed © Peter Graystone

Land is a Gift from God, The © Fr Reid Shelton Fernando

Money Comes Before Christian Values © Father George Anastacio, from *Prayers for a Change*

One Who Produces, The © Jose Costa Leite, from *Continent of Hope*

Open Our Eyes to Fairness © Kathleen Scullion/CAFOD

Our Strength and Our Help © Linda Jones/CAFOD

Prawn Farming in Bangladesh © Christian Aid

Prayer of Dedication of a Basket © Sophie Stanes/CAFOD. An extract from *Food for the Journey: A Pilgrimage*

Reflection on the Scales of Justice © Sophie Stanes/CAFOD, from *Prayers for a Change*

So Many Gifts © Wendy Whitehead

They Lost Their Livelihoods © Find Your Feet

This is Our Prayer, Cecily Taylor © Stainer and Bell Ltd

Trade and the Economy © Archbishop Diarmuid Martin

Trade for Life © Christian Aid

Way of God, The © W. L. Wallace

We Pray for the Church Throughout the World (1) © Linda Jones/ CAFOD

We Pray for the Church Throughout the World (2) © Linda Jones/ CAFOD

You Were Obese © Author Unknown/CAFOD, from *Continent of Hope*